FROM
BLACK MUSLIMS
TO
MUSLIMS:

The Transition from
Separatism to Islam,
1930-1980

by

Clifton E. Marsh

105113

The Scarecrow Press, Inc.
Metuchen, N.J., and London
1984

Excerpts in Chapter V from The Autobiography of Malcolm X, by Malcolm X with the assistance of Alex Haley (New York: Grove Press, 1964; New York: Ballantine Books, 1973, 1977) are reprinted by the permission of Random House, Inc.

The interview with Imam Wallace D. Muhammad on July 25, 1979, is printed with his permission.

Library of Congress Cataloging in Publication Data

Marsh, Clifton E., 1946–
  From black Muslims to Muslims.

  Bibliography: p.
  Includes index.
  1. Black Muslims--History. I. Title.
BP221.M37 1984   297'.87'09   84–5611
ISBN 0–8108–1705–5

In memory of my father,

CLIFTON HUGO MARSH,

my first teacher and scholar in residence.

His love, courage, wisdom and tenderness provided a role model I admire and emulate, but will never surpass.

CONTENTS

LIST OF TABLES

This work began as a purely intellectual exercise, but evolved into a human experience which has influenced the author as much as the author has shaped the book. Writing this has been a total commitment to a life-style which has taken priority over other dimensions of my life. The years (four, to be exact) of writing and revision have left me with sleepless nights, as fresh ideas subliminally seduced me into a constant restlessness.

During my research I have experienced mood, attitude, and behavior changes that have caused me often to neglect myself and family. Many times I asked, "Why am I tormenting myself and loved ones?" Each time I questioned, the answer came to me: to provide a resource for my colleagues in the academic community and the public at large which will enable them to make rational decisions about the World Community of Al-Islam in the West (WCIW). Another reason for writing this volume was to leave my imprint on the face of time so future generations will know I tried to make a contribution to the betterment of the human condition.

The collection of data for this study has taken me to the West Coast, Midwest, East Coast, and the southern region of the United States. This extensive travel allowed me to interact with, interview, and observe Muslims in their "natural state," thus providing an intimate look into the functioning of the Nation of Islam. The organization's many activities in the community gave me opportunities to observe the members' behavior frequently. Throughout the cities of the United States they were selling whiting fish and the Bilalian News as well as organizing. During the transition to Wallace D. Muhammad's leadership, I observed the Muslim

vii

community's change in dress, behavior, and perspective. This transitional period provided a unique focus for my research.

This book should interest students, scholars, and laypersons because it addresses two of the most dynamic forces in the world today: Islam and nationalism. The recent revolution in Iran and the establishment of the Islamic state, the growing Muslim population in the United States, and the Muslim-dominated Middle East penetrate our consciousness via the media each day. The primary focus of this book is not the Islamic religion, but an investigation of the origin, development, and change of the Nation of Islam from black separatism to Orthodox Islam. Elijah Muhammad led the organization for over 40 years and advocated changes through racial separatism. Since Elijah Muhammad's death on February 25, 1975, the organization changed dramatically. Under the leadership of his son Wallace D. Muhammad, the former Nation of Islam has evolved into the World Community of Al-Islam in the West.

Acknowledgments

The research began at Syracuse University, where several professors were instrumental in my growth as a scholar. Dr. Louis Kriesberg, Dr. Richard Braungart, Dr. Robert Bogdan, Dr. David Edelstein, Dr. Gunter Remmling, and Dr. Otey Scruggs were very understanding and supportive. I would like to thank the members of the WCIW for their tolerance in allowing me to investigate their life-styles and the organization. A very special thanks to Imam Wallace D. Muhammad and Public Relations secretary Hasan Shariff for providing me the opportunity to acquire an exclusive interview with the Chief Minister. * Ms. Peggy X Simmons, the curator of the Master Elijah Muhammad Library, was very helpful during my data search in New York City. I am grateful to the members of Muhammad's Mosque #24 in Richmond, Virginia, for inviting me to participate in many of their activities. Eddie 3X Jackson, Taaka Atifa Basir, and Aminah Fardan Qodir were especially helpful. Special thanks to the members of the Moorish Science Temple in Richmond, Virginia.

---

*Fictitious names were used to guarantee the privacy of rank and file Muslims interviewed. Information on Louis Farrakhan was recorded during a public address.

I also received information from the Federal Bureau of Investigation under the Freedom of Information Act. The Library of Congress, Virginia Union University Library, and the Schomburg Collection of the New York Public Library provided valuable data during my research.

Stephanie Oliverio worked very hard as an editor and spent many hours preparing my manuscript for publication. Linda Molyneaux as a typist completed the work an army of secretaries began over four years ago.

Thanks are extended to George Breathett and the Consortium on Research Training (CORT) for the research grant.

There have been many individuals who have influenced me during my life. Interaction with these people built the foundation for my present achievements. The memory of my days at Manual Arts High School in Los Angeles, California, will always kindle warmth in my heart. My three years there (1961-1964) gave me an education in "hard knocks." The people taught me not to be intimidated; it has remained the most valuable lesson of my life. Special thanks to Dr. Lawrence Jarmon, Attorney Henry S. Parks, and Dr. Harry Wells and their families. My association with Tony Wilkins, Attorney Linda Greene, Dwight Herbert, and other members of the Black Student Union nurtured my African-American consciousness. Dr. Clyde Taylor, Dr. Ora Williams, and Dr. Joe White provided intellectual and spiritual guidance which helped me through the 1960's. Louis Moore is a warm and sensitive human being; he exposed me to hours of intellectual stimulation and genuine friendship.

Finally, I would like to thank my family. My mother, Margaret Marsh, and brother, Tuck J. Hanna, always encouraged and loved me. The Pickard Family--Louise, Jerome, and Gary--was also encouraging.

A very special note of appreciation goes to my late father, Clifton Hugo Marsh, who died a few months prior to my receiving a B. A. degree. I am in debt to him for raising me by himself after the death of my mother. My father always told me, "Boy, you study before you play!" Because of his strength, dedication, courage, and love I have become the man he hoped I would.

I want my family to know their efforts were not in vain. My wife, Johnnie, and our daughter, Mecca, have paid a higher price than anyone for the completion of this

ix

book. I have been distant, moody, and uncommunicative, while Johnnie has been patient, loving, and supportive. Johnnie, above anyone else, deserves most of the credit for preserving my sanity and giving me the strength to continue. I am truly sorry for being an absentee husband in mind and body, and sincerely hope the quality of this book will heal her wounds. Johnnie and Mecca's love and encouragement made my work enjoyable because I knew that when I put down my pen, I could come home to Johnnie and Mecca. Those are the most encouraging words this writer has ever written.

This book is a sociohistorical analysis of the origin, development, and change of the Nation of Islam from black separatism to an Orthodox Islamic religious organization, the World Community of Al-Islam in the West.

Prophet Muhammad, the founder of the Islamic religion, was born in A.D. 571 in the Arabian city of Mecca. At the age of 40, Muhammad had a vision that he was visited by the angel Gabriel and received a call from God to become a prophet. Prophet Muhammad felt he could bring together the warring religious factions in the Middle East, be recognized as a prophet of Christianity, and secure a homeland for the Arab population.

Muhammad's proposal was generally rejected and he and his followers were persecuted. Muhammad traveled to Medina, 200 miles north of Mecca, and in a short time he cultivated an army, as well as a strong following of true believers in the religion that Muhammad named Islam. He established an Islamic state in Medina and returned to Mecca in A.D. 629 to establish a second Islamic republic. Mecca remains to this day the focal point for Muslims worldwide.

Muslims practice three basic principles of Islam: faith, devotional duties, and interpersonal relations. Faith consists of the theological beliefs of Islam. Devotional duties are concerned with the relationship between human beings and Allah. Interpersonal relationships are interactions among human beings on earth.

The two basic faiths in Islam are the belief in the oneness of God and the belief that Muhammad is the messenger and prophet of Allah.

The devotional duties, or "pillars of Islam," include five obligations:

1. Testimony. Muslims testify that there is no God but Allah.

2. Prayer. Muslims must face east (the direction of the Islamic Holy Land, Mecca) and pray five times daily with shoes removed. Prayers are said at dawn, noon, in the mid-afternoon, at sundown, and late in the evening.

3. Fasting. Through the month of Ramadan Muslims abstain from marital relations, eating, and drinking during the day. During the evening those restrictions are lifted.

4. Alms. Muslims pay alms to help the poor and the less fortunate of the community.

5. Pilgrimage. At least once in a lifetime each Muslim, if he/she is financially able, must make a pilgrimage to Mecca.

The Islamic religion has spread beyond Mecca and Medina to include 800 million Muslims of all races and nationalities. Islam is the dominant religion in 40 nations, primarily in Asia and Africa. The Soviet Union has over 40 million Muslims and the People's Republic of China has 17 million Muslims. There are approximately 3 million Muslims in the United States.

Most of the Muslim communities follow the "pillars," the basic beliefs, and adhere to the teachings in the Koran. There are slight alterations in practice to enable the doctrine to become compatible with various cultures. However, no Muslim community changed the doctrine, rituals, and beliefs as radically as did members of the Nation of Islam. This group was known as "Black Muslims" because the members were people of African descent practicing an unorthodox model of the Islamic religion. Founded by Wali Fard Muhammad in 1930, the organization's doctrine was a mixture of Koranic principles, the Christian Bible, his own beliefs, and those of black nationalists Marcus Garvey and Nobel Drew Ali. Fard Muhammad perceived white people as devils and black people as Muslims by nature. He advocated a separate state within the United States for African-Americans.

The organization's doctrine, rituals, and beliefs were different from those practiced by the international Islamic community. Black Muslims believed that a mere mortal was
Allah (Wali Fard Muhammad). Fard's successor, Elijah
Muhammad, spoke of himself as Allah's messenger. Clearly, those beliefs contradict the Islamic holy book, the Koran.

    The Nation of Islam was not primarily a religious
body, but a social movement organization designed to alleviate socioeconomic problems of the African-American.
African-Americans are subjected to an unequal distribution
of rewards, political power and opportunities, which systematically restricts their life chances to succeed as a
group. By organizing in a collective movement, African-
Americans want to change conditions which foster racial and
class inequality. African-Americans are unique in American society, being immigrants not by choice but by force.
Therefore, the crucial question facing African-American
leadership is, how can former slaves achieve equality within
a capitalist economy and predominantly white society?
African-Americans have sought numerous methods to achieve
economic equality, political power, and social respect. Most
black people have accepted Christianity and have identified
themselves as Americans, often using Christianity as a vehicle for social reform.

    There have been several periods in African-American
history when integration appeared improbable and equity within the economic order was impossible. During these periods
African-Americans have sought counterculture methods to
create social and political changes. One of these methods
is black nationalism; it is a collective effort by people of
African descent to overcome cultural, economic, and political exploitation. Black separatism is one aspect of nationalism which includes territorial separatism ("a nation within a
nation") or emigration ("back to Africa").

    The Nation of Islam was a religious separatist organ-
ization. Its founder, Wali Fard, and his successor, Elijah
Muhammad, believed the African population residing in America could never achieve freedom, justice, and equality as citizens of the United States. They advocated a separate black
nation where people of African descent would have the power
to govern their own affairs of state.

    The concept of separatism is almost as old as the
African presence in the United States. As early as 1815

Paul Cuffee wanted to emigrate to Africa. In 1858 Henry Highland Garnet created the African Civilization Society to establish a state in West Africa. Martin Delaney merged his National Emigration Conference with Garnet's organization in 1861 to promote emigration to the Niger Valley. The brilliant scholar Edward Wilmont Blyden, a West Indian, emigrated to Monrovia in 1851 and advocated Islam as a qualitative change from Christianity. In 1916 Marcus Garvey, through his Universal Negro Improvement Association, attracted over one million recruits for emigration to Africa.

The attraction to Africa or a separate African-American state has always been accompanied by extremely oppressive conditions in the United States. When analyzed, U.S. economic and political conditions provided the push toward separatism more than Africa or a separate state "pulled" black Americans.

The Nation of Islam began as a separatist movement between 1914 and 1930, when the social conditions were unusually oppressive, creating discontent among people of African descent in the United States. During World War I increased work opportunities caused a migration to the North, the "promised land," and raised the hopes of African-Americans that equity was possible within the economic order. However, when the war was over, returning soldiers were hired and many black workers lost their jobs. The race riots of 1919, the racist treatment black soldiers received, and the Depression heightened their discontent and alienation. These socioeconomic conditions made the climate conducive to the appeals of a race leader.

Wali Fard Muhammad began the Nation of Islam during this period when black people were susceptible to his doctrine. Fard Muhammad was employed as a peddler selling merchandise in the Detroit black community. His role as peddler enabled him to enter people's homes. Once inside, he began to propagate what he called the "natural religion" for the black man, Islam. Gradually the word spread about his teachings and he held meetings in various homes throughout the community. One night an unemployed auto worker named Elijah Poole attended one of Fard's sermons. Poole was mesmerized by Fard and became his follower. Upon his conversion he received the name Elijah Muhammad.

Elijah Muhammad assumed leadership of the organization in 1934. He led the organization for 41 years until his death on February 25, 1975. His son, Wallace D. Muhammad, succeeded him and began to change the leadership, organizational structure, and doctrine to coincide with Orthodox Islam. Wallace D. Muhammad's leadership ushered in a new era for what had become the most misunderstood, powerful, and feared black separatist organization in the United States.

Chapter I

BLACK NATIONALISM AS A SOCIAL MOVEMENT

The objectives of this chapter are to develop a social movement framework in order to analyze the socioeconomic conditions that make it conducive for a black nationalist movement to emerge and to discuss the black nationalist perspective in the United States.

Black nationalism has been a consistent theme throughout the history of the African presence in America. Black
nationalism had become a viable change mechanism when
African-Americans perceived the social, economic, and political conditions in the United States to be intolerable and in-
flexible to change by traditional means.

The problem for over twenty million African-Americans
is, How can former slaves achieve equality within a capitalist
economy and a predominantly white society? People of African descent are subjected to unequal distribution of rewards,
political power, and opportunities, which systematically restricts their life chances to succeed as a group. By organizing in a social movement, African-Americans want to change
the conditions of racial and class inequality.

SOCIAL MOVEMENT DEFINITION

A social movement is a large, organized group of people committed to collective goals and ideals to preserve or change the
existing political-economic structure and human relations in
society. This definition distinguishes social movements from
other groups and group activities, such as lobbies, crowds,
and tactics.

Lobby

A lobby is an organized group exerting political, economic, and ideological pressure within traditional channels to influence the public legislative process in order to create policy sympathetic to the group's interests.

Crowd Activity

Riots, panic, and mob behavior are spontaneous, unorganized, and leaderless. Individuals do not consciously join these kinds of activities to achieve specific goals, nor are they sustained to change political and economic institutions.

Tactics

Tactics are defined as interaction by groups of people to bring their grievances to the attention of the public and governing elites. Demonstrations, rallies, and boycotts are organized to achieve the goals of the movement.

Social movements are concerned with changing the power relationships and the basic socioeconomic institutions. Individuals organize to improve their status as a group in society. People join movements for "... some kind of change to be achieved, some innovation to be made or a previous condition to be restored."[1]

UNDERLYING ASSUMPTIONS

There are several underlying assumptions associated with the social movement definition. Movements are organized and have a structure; there is a consciousness shared among individuals that their socioeconomic problems can be solved more effectively in groups. The solution to social problems is believed to lie in the preservation of or a change in the means of production and governance of the society. Four areas will be covered in the following discussion: the economic order, class, minority group status, and the political order.

The Economic Order

In our definition of a social movement, one underlying

assumption is that certain groups in society are dissatisfied
with their economic status and the governance of society.
The motivation for the creation of a social movement is often
found in the economic order.

The economic order is the system a society uses to
produce and distribute goods and services. The forces of
production include natural resources, expertise, tools, and
labor. The interaction of individuals in this process is called
the relations of production.

The United States is a capitalist society, which means
the ownership of the means of production and distribution are
operated for profit. The wealth derived from the profit is
controlled by an elite class, which is comprised of a small
segment of the total population. The members of the elite
class create corporations to safeguard their economic interests. The corporations are "... administratively and politically interrelated; together [they] hold the keys to economic
decisions."[2] A "Capitalist society contains groups that are
unequal in their participation in the productive system. As
in all class societies, there is a dominant class that appro-
priates a surplus produced by a subordinate class."[3]

In the system of stratification, individuals are placed
in the class system according to their occupation in the division of labor. The occupation represents different life chances
to acquire income, property, higher education, and job opportunities. The primary components of the stratification
system are occupation, economic class, social prestige and
power. An occupation represents a marketable skill and a
specific function in the division of labor.

Occupation is the link between the individual, the class
system, status and power, "... as well as to skill and function; to understand the occupations composing any social stra-
tum, we must consider them in terms of each of these interrelated dimensions."[4]

Since the production of goods is less expensive than
the workers' wages, this creates surplus wealth, or profit,
for the employer. When surplus wealth is not distributed
equally among various groups in society, a system of inequality emerges. The unequal groups are classes composed
of people with different access to social rewards and opportunities by virtue of their rank in the economic order. A
class "... is a set of people who share similar life choices

because of their similar class situations."[5] The "... combination of the division of labor with super and subordination
makes up that basic configuration of social positions, strata
and classes in the social system."[6] The individuals in the
subordinate classes sell their skills and talent in the labor
market and "... in these occupations men work for someone
else on someone else's property."[7]

The Working Class

Individuals who own no segments of the means of production and have no controlling voice in the governing of society comprise the working class. Members of the working
class trade their skills, talent, and labor for a wage paid by
the employers. Traditionally, white collar workers have been
the economic buffer between the working class and the economic elite.

The white collar worker is in a similar property-class
position as the blue collar worker. White collar workers
"... have no direct fiscal tie to the means of production, no
prime claims upon the proceeds from property. Like factory
workers, they work for those who do own such means of live-
lihood."[8] The working class in the United States is comprised
of four main segments: 1) blue collar workers, which include
semi-skilled and skilled workers; 2) white collar workers,
which include clericals, professional, and technical individuals and sales managers; 3) proprietors of small business,
owners of "Mom and Pop" stores or small business ventures
that employ few or no employees, and physicians in private
practice; and 4) reserve labor force, which includes unskilled
and unemployed members of society. Members of this fourth
group have limited opportunities and lack skills, hence they
are always on the fringe of the labor market.

Minority Group Status

Minority group individuals, by virtue of unique physical
or cultural characteristics that differ from the dominant racial,
ethnic, or religious group, are subjected to different and unequal treatment and become victims of collective institutional
discrimination. The presence of a minority group in society
implies the existence of a corresponding dominant group with
higher social status and greater privileges. Minority status
carries with it the exclusion from full participation in life of
society.[9]

Once a person of African descent achieves a better economic status, that person is denied the social rewards which normally accompany upward mobility. C. Wright Mills said, "Prestige involves two persons: one to claim it and another to honor the claim." Minority group status is not honored in the United States. Middle-class and professional blacks are subject to the same social ostracism as working class and poor blacks in a society which treats them equally in the prestige system. Prestige is often a birth right; the black child, regardless of individual achievement, "... will not receive the deference which the white child may successfully claim. Race, nationality and family prestige is based on, or at least limited by, descent."[10]

Political Order

The political order is controlled by a segment of the population called the governing elite. The Marxist term "ruling class" applies only to an economic fact that small groups of people own large sums of wealth; the term does not address military and political power.

The modern governing elite in the United States is comprised of the economic elite, leaders of the military, and government officials. The power to make "... decisions of national and international consequences are now so clearly seated in political, military and economic institutions, that other areas of society seem off to the side, and on occasion, readily subordinated to these."[11] The modern state is large and complicated, "however, it still has the same core function to be a machine for insuring a smooth transfer of wealth from a producing class to an appropriating class."[12] The governing elite controls production of ideas through the major institutions in society, such as religious institutions, school systems, mass media, judicial systems, and government agencies. These institutions reinforce the ideas that are compatible with the interest of the governing elite, define what behavior is legitimate, and establish the norms for individuals to emulate. The ideologies the state produces "... tend to explain and justify the existing class structure."[13]

Most members of the working class fulfill their economic role with little awareness of how it affects their social status, class and interpersonal relations. In order for individuals to be organized, there must be a common consciousness shared by the group that their individual socio-economic problems are a result of the economic order and

manipulation by the governing elite. There are certain social
conditions which "... encourage people to change their view
of themselves and their world, to object to and challenge ar-
rangements which they may have accepted previously."[14]

SOCIAL CHANGE

Social Conditions

Economic inequality and institutional racism benefit
white workers and are socioeconomic obstacles to proletariat
unity. This structural relationship encourages competition
within the working class which escalates into racial conflict.
"The white groups tend to view their interests in a particu-
larly united way when confronted with blacks making demands
which are seen as threatening to vested interests."[15]   The
coalition between major corporations and the American labor
movement has effectively co-opted and institutionalized the
leadership to reinforce the interest of the economic elite.
These socioeconomic realities have forced black leaders to
organize around racial issues versus class solidarity.

Historically, black nationalist movements have occurred
during periods of change in society, such as migration, a
changing job market, and during wars. "Only in wartime,
have labor shortages been sufficiently severe to induce employers to open up previously closed occupations to blacks
and to provide employment to many black youths and women
[who had been unable] to get regular jobs."[16]

Social changes in the United States create a push-pull
effect. The push is the social, political, and economic conditions in the United States. The pull is the attraction to
Africa as a homeland. "Changes in political behavior and
beliefs do not occur separately from economic change."[17]
The gradual increase in the standard of living ferments a
sense of optimism. When economic, political, and social
conditions do not continue to improve as expected, individuals
become frustrated, and anger and discontent arise.

The social conditions previously discussed raise the
expectations of blacks that equality and political power are
attainable in the United States. When they are not achieved,
the attraction to Africa becomes a possible solution. If the
"... deprived can readily see who is responsible for their
condition, that group may soon be defined as the enemy and
becomes the focus for the discontent."[18]

Group Consciousness

Changes in an individual's consciousness are a result of transformation in the society; "... it accompanies reorganization of the individual's life situation as a result of and in response to structural transformation. It profoundly affects an individual's personality and world view."[19]

A political mentality or group consciousness is affected by the person's position in stratified systems. A group consciousness is likely to occur among homogeneous groups in regard to class, occupation, and prestige. The majority of blacks work in low-paying occupations, creating similar interests, working conditions, and life chances. The economic position allows them frequent communication to discuss grievances. Social isolation, as residents of segregated communities and minority status, add to this cohesiveness. By living under similar conditions, blacks "... begin to seek a similarity of interest with one another, interaction among them intensifies; they start to share a common perspective and group consciousness emerges."[20] African-American minority group status and economic deprivation become the basis for political action.

ORGANIZATION

Leadership

Integrationist leaders representing "traditional" civil rights organizations are often responsive to corporate interests and not the needs of the black masses. The co-optation of leaders hinders any attempt to relieve the grievances of the black community. This kind of leadership benefits the status of certain individuals, "... but it does not speak to the alleviation of the multitude of social problems shared by the masses."[21] Professional blacks are subjects of political powerlessness similar to their working class or unemployed brethren. Institutional racism and economic inequality place a limit on black upward mobility and the number of black people to fill roles in the division of labor. The precarious socioeconomic status of being black and middle class motivates some blacks to become dissidents and leaders of nationalist movements. The "... intellectual elite deserving radical social change must depend on the deprived masses for support by aligning his interest with that of the masses; [through this move] strong impetus for change is affected."[22]

The "... leaders encourage group members to question the present distribution of social goods and legitimacy of existing authority structure and they work out practical means for attaining the goal."[23] Organizations usually have a charismatic leader, an organizer, and an intellectual. All three types have unique functions within the organization, but charismatic leadership attracts the masses. The charismatic leader appeals to the emotions and ideals of the alienated. He or she leads by the pure force of his/her personality, "... by virtue of which he/she was set apart from ordinary men and treated as endowed with supernatural superhuman powers."[24]

Ideology

The charismatic leader is able to articulate an ideology which offers political solutions to socioeconomic problems. An ideology is a belief system that provides a world view which reinforces the cause of a particular class or group. It is "... a coherent set of ideas and guidelines for altering the authority structure."[25] The ideology organizes individuals into a cohesive body and enables the movement to overcome socioeconomic differences; that is, age, class, regional, race, and religious differences. Individuals join a social movement because "... it offers answers to certain dissatisfactions prompted by societal conditions in relation to their unique experiences."[26]

The ideology provides a perspective for individuals to link personal injustice to institutional inequality thereby encouraging commitment to the organization's goals. The organization provides protection, security, sense of identity, and economic well-being.

Large groups of individuals and economic resources are valuable tools to attack social problems by rational means. Each individual is assigned specific functions and everyone's role is clearly defined; organization enables the group to pursue its objectives.

TYPES OF SOCIAL MOVEMENTS

There are five basic types of social movements which vary according to goals and objectives: 1) revolutionary movements, 2) reform movements, 3) backlash movements, 4) apolitical movements, and 5) separatist movements. People of African descent have participated in a majority of these movements, adding a black perspective to accommodate their unique socioeconomic problems. A black nationalist social movement is an organized effort to create a collective consciousness and racial/cultural pride, and it may or may not desire to control a sovereign territory. Some nationalists acknowledge that blacks have similar economic, political, and social problems as a group, but they have no desire to have a separate state or emigrate to Africa. All separatists are nationalists but not all nationalists believe in separatism.

African-American nationalists have taken two basic stands: First, some nationalists have a psychic identity with Africa, but desire to remain in America. These individuals may or may not desire land within the United States (a nation within a nation). Second, other nationalists feel freedom cannot be achieved in America and desire to emigrate to Africa. In the framework of previous discussions, black nationalism can now be defined as an "ideological formulation, i.e., subjective reconstruction of reality in black terms; a social strategy containing proposals and programs of reconstruction and a collective vocation, that is, a struggle for community."[27]

An examination of black nationalism shows that it is a body of political thought and behavior, ranging from simple expressions of racial solidarity to the more sophisticated ideologies of Pan-Africanism. Between these extremes lie many varieties of black nationalism.

Revolutionary Movements

Revolutionary movements are concerned with overturning present governing elite and seizing control of the state in order to change the means of production and the redistribution of wealth in society.

Revolutionary black nationalists perceive the black communities as colonies in the United States. These colonies should be organized and serve as the vanguard force to overthrow the existing political and economic order, thereby bringing about liberation for all oppressed people. Revolutionary nationalists perceive the African-American community as a nation, but politically do not control its destiny. Such nationalists as Huey P. Newton and Bobby Seale, founders of the Black Panther Party, proclaimed African-Americans must identify with people of color throughout the world as an international majority instead of an American minority. Revolutionary nationalists perceived the economic and racial problems in America to be linked with the international problems of imperialism, colonialism, and exploitation of foreign labor and natural resources.

The revolutions of Third World people in China, Angola, Mozambique, Cuba, Algiers, and Vietnam encouraged the nationalists to suggest that African-Americans align themselves with these people as comrades in an international struggle against racism and capitalism.

Reform Movements

Reform movements would like the distribution of wealth and governance of society to remain the same. They are concerned with manipulating specific institutions, attitudes, or laws which deny them access to social rewards and privileges.

Cultural Nationalism. Cultural nationalists feel blacks represent a distinct and separate culture from that of the white society. It is this cultural link with other blacks which forms a major portion of the ideology. Glorification of African art, literature, philosophy and history are essential to liberate the Afro-psyche from the traditions of Western Civilization. Also, the assertion of a distinct life-style and world view in such ways as assuming African or Arabic names, wearing African clothes, and speaking African languages is essential to becoming free.

Cultural nationalists believe racial pride in themselves as a group comes before political change. They advocate creating black institutions, rituals, and holidays to celebrate black unity and African heritage.

The cultural nationalists "... are concerned with returning to the old African culture, thereby regaining their identity and freedom. In other words, they feel that the African culture will automatically bring political freedom."[28]

Religious Nationalism. Religious nationalists perceive religion as a viable change mechanism. They perceive Christ or Muhammad as black leaders of non-white people against the rule of white nations.

One of the most dynamic black nationalists was Edward W. Blyden, born in 1832 in St. Thomas, Virgin Islands. He emigrated to Liberia on January 26, 1851. Blyden is significant because he was the earliest nationalist thinker to articulate a definite black nationalist ideology. Blyden's influence covers politics (back to Africa), economics (African socialism), and religion (urged the belief in Islam). Blyden worked and lived in Liberia for over 40 years as a teacher, builder of educational institutions, and political leader. Blyden was the first nationalist to combine a "back to Africa" theme with African socialism and Islam as a religion to create African unity. Blyden concluded, "... that Christianity, which focused on changing African values, had destructive and deleterious influence on Africans. He considered Islam more appropriate to the basic African life-style."[29] Blyden encouraged exchange and cooperation with Islamic states of Africa with the mutual aim of incorporating them into the Negro Republic.[30]

Blyden learned and instructed his students in Arabic and urged them to work as emissaries to Islamic nations.

Economic Nationalism. Economic nationalists advocate controlling the community's economic interest by establishing business enterprises. They may call for cooperative or capitalist ownership; the central theme is that community control of business enterprises is essential to the real development and growth of the community itself.

Pan-Africanism. Pan-Africanism is a movement toward economic cooperation, cultural awareness, and international political solidarity among people of African descent.

W. E. B. Du Bois was instrumental in developing Pan-Africanism. Du Bois and Henry Sylvester Williams protested European colonization of Africa through the Pan-African Congress held in 1900, 1921, 1923, 1927, and 1945. The conferences articulated several concerns: colonization of Africa, human rights in southern Africa, exploitation of blacks living in predominantly white societies, and self-government for nations in the West Indies.

The Pan-African Congress fostered the idea that "... various groups of Africans, quite separate in origin, became so united in experience and so exposed to the impact of new cultures that they began to think of Africa as one idea and one land."[31]

Backlash Movements

These movements develop as a result of progressive changes in the society. Individuals join to resist change and maintain the existing social, economic, and political relationships. People of African descent have been victimized by backlash movements, which often emerge when blacks and other minorities appear to be making progress. The Ku Klux Klan, John Birch Society, and American Nazi Party are examples of backlash movements.

Apolitical Movements

Apolitical movements are not concerned with economic inequality or political power in society. There is a release of tension, collective flight, and self-expression with no plans to change the existing social order.

Historically, religious-oriented "pie in the sky" type organizations like "Father Divine," "Sweet Daddy Grace," and Reverend Ike have offered solutions to economic and political oppression through prayer and ceremonies. Apolitical movements help people cope and adapt to the situation instead of changing it.

Separatist Movements

Separatism is the belief that people of African descent cannot attain freedom and equality in the United States, therefore, the solution is to acquire a separate state. There are two forms of separatism: (a) territorial separatism (nation within a nation) and (b) the back-to-Africa movement.

Territorial Separatism. Organizations such as the Nation of Islam and the Republic of New Africa have asked for territory within the boundaries of the United States, a nation within a nation.

Nationalists of this persuasion feel oppressed in the United States, but have no strong inclination to emigrate to Africa. The nation within a nation concept depends upon the economic and military support as well as goodwill of the parent nation (United States). Territorial separatists assume the parent nation and the black states could coexist peacefully without exploitation by the dominant power.

Emigration, Back to Africa. A consistent and strong theme in African-American social thought has been the conclusion that blacks could never achieve equality in America and the only solution is to leave. Emigration has been viewed as an alternative when the American ideal of equality seemed unattainable. There was more of a dissatisfaction with the American society than there was a desire to live in Africa.

Marcus Garvey was the leader of a return-to-Africa movement. He founded the Universal Negro Improvement Association in 1916. Garvey planned to transplant the black American community in Africa, but the emigration theme did not originate with Garvey.

Paul Cuffee was an influential emigrationist. Cuffee wanted to transport black farmers, mechanics, and artisans to Sierra Leone and establish commercial and political intercourse with African states. With $4,000 of his own funds, Cuffee transported 38 African-Americans to Sierra Leone in 1815. The American colonization society was founded four years after Cuffee's death in 1821. The first settlement was called Monrovia in honor of President Monroe.

In 1858 Henry Highland Garnet became president of the African Civilization Society. Its goal was to establish in West Africa, "... a grand center of negro nationality from which shall flow the streams of commercial, intellectual and political power which shall make colored people everywhere respected."[32]

Martin R. Delaney merged his National Emigration Conference with Garnet's African Civilization Society in May 1861 to raise funds to promote resettlement in the Niger Valley. Martin Delaney felt black Americans were culturally unique, "... as the Poles in Russia, the Hungarians in Austria, the Welsh, Irish and Scotch in the British dominions."[33] The ambitious plans of Garnet and Delaney were stalled by the Civil War; they felt if blacks participated in the war it would uplift their status as a group.

Edward Wilmont Blyden, a West Indian, migrated to Monrovia in 1851. Blyden firmly believed blacks could never be equal to whites in the United States. Blyden was very critical of American blacks for delaying emigration plans in hopes of achieving equality in the United States. He said, "Half the time and energy that will be spent by them in struggles against caste, if devoted to the building up of a

home and nationality of their own, would produce results im-
measurably more useful and satisfactory. "[34]

Blyden performed extensive research on Africa, its
people and the culture.   Blyden was the first black nationalist
to investigate the economic base of the African social systems.   Blyden concluded it was "socialistic, cooperative and
equitable an ideal for which Europe was desperately striving
as the answers to the ills created by individualism and un-
scrupulous competition."[35]   These ideas place Blyden above
all nationalists before him or since.   Blyden lived in Africa;
studied the society; and incorporated Islam, African Socialism, and emigration in his world view.

Blyden's world view and self-esteem were not influenced by the flux of the economic marketplace.   Nationalists
from the United States (such as Cuffee, Garnet, and Delaney)
felt driven out of America by oppressive conditions rather
than a desire to live in Africa.   This strong attraction to
Africa is what separated Blyden and Marcus Garvey from
other nationalists.

ORGANIZATION TRANSFORMATION

The transformation of the Nation of Islam to the World Community of Al-Islam in the West is consistent with the general
trend of social movement development.   There are three
stages associated with the transformation: the formation
stage (organization founded by Wali Fard Muhammad), the
formalization stage (development of ideology and institutions
by Elijah Muhammad), and traditionalization (the change from
separatism to Islam by Wallace D. Muhammad).

During the formation stage of a movement, social
conditions create perilous circumstances in which individuals
seek a solution by following a charismatic leader.   When the
movement attains a social and economic base, the charismatic leader depends less on charisma and more on a bu-
reaucratic structure.   The creation of a formal bureaucracy
is the beginning of the formalization stage.   During this stage
Elijah Muhammad succeeded Wali Fard as the "Messenger of
Allah" and began to create a distinct black separatist doctrine and a formal bureaucracy.   Elijah Muhammad's death
on February 25, 1975, was the start of the traditionalization
stage.

Wallace D. Muhammad succeeded his father as leader of the Nation of Islam. He changed its name to the World Community of Al-Islam in the West. The name change is more than symbolic; it reflects an alteration in structure, doctrine, rituals, leadership and goals. The traditionalization stage under Wallace D. Muhammad is a "... diffusion of goals, in which a pragmatic leadership replaces unattainable goals." This stage is "... always in the direction of greater conservatism."[36] The leadership during this stage usually revises the goals to accommodate the dominant group. Elijah Muhammad wanted to establish a nation within a nation, although this was almost impossible to attain in the United States. Wallace Muhammad is trying to achieve more realistic goals, such as ideological reform (within the organization), restoration of urban areas through employment, and trade with Islamic governments.

This chapter has outlined the economic and political system in the United States. It can be concluded that the structure of inequality is not enough to motivate certain groups in society to join a social movement. Certain periods in history are more conducive to rebellion than others. For example, Wali Fard Muhammad's presence in Detroit during the Depression enabled him to capitalize on the discontent experienced by many African-Americans.

A significant number of the early converts of the Nation of Islam were recent migrants from the southern section of the United States. The new migrants became potential recruits when their expectations of economic mobility and political power were not met.

Chapter II is an analysis of American social conditions between 1914 and 1930. We shall see why international and domestic conditions prompted many African-Americans to investigate separatism as a solution to inequality in the United States.

NOTES

1. Rudolph Heberle, Social Movements (New York: Appleton-Century-Crofts, 1951), p. 6.

2. C. Wright Mills, Power, Politics and People (New York: Ballantine Books, 1963), p. 28.

3. Roberta Ash-Garner, Social Movements in America (Chicago: Rand-McNally, 1977), p. 17

4. Mills, Power, p. 307.

5. Ibid.

6. Anthony Oberschall, Social Conflict and Social Movements (Englewood Cliffs, N.J.: Prentice-Hall, 1973), p. 33.

7. Mills, Power, p. 307.

8. Ibid., p. 308.

9. George E. Simpson and Milton J. Yinger, Racial and Cultural Minorities (New York: Harper and Row, 1965), p. 16.

10. Mills, Power, p. 311.

11. Ibid, p. 27.

12. Roberta Ash-Garner, Social Movements, p. 4.

13. Ibid.

14. Irving Krauss, Stratification Class and Conflict (New York: The Free Press, 1976), p. 21.

15. Charles V. Hamilton and Stokely Carmichael, Black Power (New York: Vintage Books, 1967), p. 7.

16. Victor Perlo, Economics of Racism U.S.A. (New York: International Publishers, 1975), p. 56.

17. Roberta Ash-Garner, Social Change (Chicago: Rand-McNally, 1977), p. vii.

18. Krauss, Stratification, p. 21.

19. Ash-Garner, Social Change, p. 47.

20. Krauss, Stratification, p. 16.

21. Hamilton and Carmichael, Black Power, p. 12.

22. Ron E. Roberts and Robert M. Kloss, Social Movements (Saint Louis, Mo.: V.I. Mosby Company, 1974), p. 177.

23. Krauss, Stratification, p. 22.

24. Max Weber, The Theory of Social and Economic Organization (New York: Oxford University Press, 1977), p. 358.

25. Krauss, Stratification, p. 22.

26. Raymond Hall, Black Separatism and Social Reality (New York: Pergamon Press, 1977), p. 13.

27. M. Ron Karenga, "Afro-American Nationalism, Beyond Mystification and Misconception," Black Books Bulletin, Vol. 6, No. 1 (Spring 1979), p. 15.

28. Roberts and Kloss, Social Movements, p. 47.

29. James Turner, "Blyden, Black Nationalism and Emigration Schemes," Black Books Bulletin, Vol. 6, No. 1 (Spring 1979), p. 25.

30. Hollis Lynch, Edward Wilmont Blyden (London: Oxford Press, 1967), p. 46.

31. W.E.B. Du Bois, The World and Africa (New York: Viking Press, 1947), p. 7.

32. Lynch, Blyden, pp. 23-24.

33. Martin D. Delaney, The Condition, Elevation, Emigration and Destiny of the Colored People of the United States, Politically Considered (New York: Arno Press, 1968), Appendix.

34. Lynch, Blyden, p. 35.

35. Ibid.

36. Joseph H. Gusfield, Protest, Reform and Revolt (New York: John Wiley and Sons, 1970), p. 110.

Chapter II

SOCIAL CONDITIONS, 1914-1930

Social movements arise in society during periods of social change. The period 1914-1930 represents one of the most dynamic periods in the history of the United States.

Social conditions that provoked discontent among blacks were World War I and the Depression. They caused migration of blacks to the North and race riots following World War I. When conditions were improving during this era, African-Americans expected their status to continue to improve. When they experienced a drop in status after the war, frustration, anxiety, and discontent arose. During this era African-Americans improved their status, but relative to the white population they did not improve at all. This disparity between the two groups remains the same today, thereby retarding attempts for equality within the work force and society in general.

With the arrival of World War I blacks were confronted with a question concerning citizenship in the United States. Should they help save democracy in France while they were denied participation in the democratic process in Alabama and New York City?

African-Americans' confidence in the government to improve the group's status in the military was bolstered when the Wilson Administration appointed Emmett J. Scott, Negro Advisor to the Secretary of War. Scott has been a confidential secretary to Booker T. Washington for 18 years. His functions were to urge equal and impartial application of the selective service system and to create programs that promoted morale among black soldiers and civilians as well.

Black men fought bravely against tremendous physical and psychological odds to prove their loyalty as Americans and their valor as soldiers.   However, in the face of all practical evidence prior to, during, and after World War I, there were widespread stereotypes restricting blacks' participation in the U.S. military.

The United States' involvement in World War I required massive recruitment in order to succeed.   Congress passed and President Wilson signed the Selective Service Law on May 18, 1917, which required all able-bodied American men between 21 and 31 years old to register with their local draft boards.

The draft consumed some of the best possible labor and "... there is little doubt of southern reluctance to have black farm labor drafted.   In fact, it was a not uncommon policy for draft boards to take blacks who owned their own land while exempting those who worked for white sharecroppers or tenants."[1]   Draft boards

> ... regularly inducted blacks who were physically unfit while excluding whites with similar disabilities.   Blacks entitled to a deferment were railroaded into the army, while whites with no legitimate excuse for exemption were allowed to escape the requirements of the draft system.[2]

There were 404,384 black troops in the military--most were in the Army.   Out of these were 1,353 commissioned officers trained in segregated facilities.   Tables I and II (on pages 27 and 28) reveal the differences in selective service classifications and inductions comparing white with black.   In Table I, Class I included those men available for active duty.   Deferred status included those who were exempt from military service.

Out of a total of 10,640,846 people registered for the draft, blacks comprised 10.13 percent, or 1,078,331 blacks registered for the draft from June 5, 1917, to September 11, 1918.   Of the 1,078,331 blacks registered, 556,917 were ranked for Class I; that is, 51.65 percent of the black men examined were fit for military service.   There were 521,414 blacks who received military deferments, which made 48.35 percent of the black men ineligible for military duty.   Compared with white men, 9,562,515 registered for the draft during the same time period and 3,110,659 were given the Class I status, which made only 32.53 percent of the whites ineligible for the draft, while 6,541,856 were deferred, which made 67.4 percent of the white men who were registered ineligible for military service.

TABLE I:

Black and White Classifications Compared

Total Black and Whites Registered	Number	Percent of Classified
June 5, 1917-Sept. 11, 1918	10,640,846	--
Total Black Registered	1,078,331	100.00
Class I	556,917	51.65
Deferred Classes	521,414	48.35
Total White Registered	9,562,515	100.00
Class I	3,110,659	32.53
Deferred Classes	6,451,856	67.47

Percentage Accepted for Service
(Calls Before December 15, 1917)

Black	36.23
White	24.75

Source: Second report of the Provost Marshal General to the Secretary of War on the Operations of the Selective System to December 20, 1918. Washington, D.C.: Government Printing Office, 1919.

Blacks accepted for service comprised 36.23 percent, while 24.75 percent of the whites were called for active duty. These data apparently amazed Emmett Scott; he offered the following criticism: "The Provost Marshal offered more or less elaborate explanations of the reasons for the higher figures for colored registrants in Class I, but they do not seem now, to be tenable reasons."[3]

TABLE II:

Black and White Inductions Compared

Total Black and White Inductions	Number	Percent of Inductions
June 5, 1912-Nov. 11, 1918	2,810,296	100.00
Black	367,710	13.08
White	2,442,586	86.92

Source: Second report of the Provost Marshal General to the Secretary of War on the Operations of the Selective Service System to December 20, 1918. Washington, D.C.: Government Printing Office, 1919.

In Table II, out of the 2,810,296 people drafted, 367,710 were black, which is 13.08 percent of the total inductions for the period of June 5, 1912, to November 11, 1918. Blacks comprised less than 10 percent of the total population, but were 13 percent of the inducted military force.

Along with the discriminatory practices of the draft policy in World War I, "... intelligence testing was a new tool of the new science of psychology: in fact, the massing of men of war gave psychologists their real chance to develop and validate the test."[4]

These tests, seemingly scientific, helped "validate" blacks' inferiority as a race and incompetence as fighting men. The army assigned blacks to stevedore regiments and labor battalions because it was commonly believed that blacks were only suited for manual labor.

Discrimination by the United States government was
clear. Out of approximately 350,000 blacks drafted, only
40,000 became combat soldiers. Blacks inducted into the
armed services were segregated from white soldiers during
their training and they also experienced segregation during
active duty.

The induction of blacks as fighting men created the
unique problem of who would lead them. The American government had the answer: white men, of course! In the following government document, the leadership of the 92nd division was appointed:

> October 24, the War Department establishes the
> 92nd Div., National Army; colored selective ser-
> vice men from the United States at large are to
> be organized into the component units at various
> northern stations. General and field officers in
> the technical branches and in the field artillery
> above the grade of first lieutenant are to be white."[5]

The army made a concerted effort to exclude blacks from
the Officers' ranks. Through the efforts of the National Association for the Advancement of Colored People (NAACP) and
various pressure groups, a compromise was created to train
and recruit black officers.

There were fourteen training camps for whites, and
in conjunction with the government's policy on segregation,
a separate training camp was created for blacks. Led by
Joel Spingarn, President of the NAACP, and James Weldon
Johnson, a leading NAACP official,

> ... a central committee of Negro college men to
> seek officer training opportunities was formed, with
> headquarters at Howard University in Washington,
> D.C. One thousand Negro college students pledged
> themselves to enter officers training camp for Ne-
> groes, which accommodated 1,250 men and was
> formally opened at Des Moines, Iowa.[6]

Even though the government trained these troops and officers,
their role as efficient fighting personnel was played down during the conflict. Many of these black officers were not given
an opportunity to lead their men. After a short time in combat they were usually replaced by white officers. Efficiency

boards were created to weed out black officers.   Such boards
could act on the mere opinion of a field officer.

    The majority of the inefficiency charges by these
boards were based on "race and nature" and not on imcom-
petence of the individual officer.

    The first African-Americans to arrive in France were
the labor battalions comprising approximately 150,000 men.
Most of the combat officers and troops served in the all-
black 92nd and 93rd Infantry Divisions.   The 93rd Division
consisted of all-black national guard units, the 9th-Illinois,
the 15th-New York, units from the District of Columbia,
Maryland, Ohio, Tennessee, and Massachusetts.   The Division never functioned as a military unit and was forced into
action by the severe need for reinforcements in the French
army.   The 93rd Division landed in France on January 1,
1918, and was integrated into the French army.   Equipped
as French units,

         ... carrying French rifles and eating French ra-
         tions, they knew an equality denied them by their
         own military.   They operated in the area of Meuse
         Argonne near Saint Mihiel Champagne and in the
         Oise-Aisne Offensive from the early summer of
         1918 to the end of the war. [7]

The men of the 93rd distinguished themselves in battle and
540 officers and men were decorated by American and French
governments.   The 93rd Division suffered 2,583 casualties of
which 574 were killed and 2,009 wounded.

    The 92nd was unprepared for combat.   The Division
trained in sections and never assembled as a whole unit until
the last days of the war.   It was given "... the most ignor-
ant and physically disqualified Negroes in the United States,
with 40 percent of its men illiterate.   Its white officers were
unsympathetic to the Negro men and hostile to the Negro officers."[8]

    The most alarming note of institutional discrimination
by the United States Government occurred during August of
1918.   The General Headquarters of the American Army at
Chaiemont, the French military mission, sent out racist
propaganda to French governors and mayors where black
troops were stationed.   The document, entitled "Secret Information Concerning Black American Troops," concerned

the American attitude toward blacks, "... warning against
social recognition, stating that Negroes were prone to deeds
of violence and were threatening America with degeneration.
The white troops backed this propaganda by warnings and
tales wherever they preceded the blacks. "[9]

The effort by the United States government to dis-
credit black troops in the eyes of the French was unsuccess-
ful. The French government saw fit to look out for the welfare of the black soldiers. Generally, blacks moved about
freely in France without rigid social barriers. The real
concern of the U.S. government underlying the "secret document" was that the humane treatment blacks received would
turn them bitter toward American racism when they returned
home. To reinforce the subordinate behavior expected of
black soldiers upon their return to America, the Secretary
of War sent Robert R. Moton, successor to Booker T. Washington at Tuskegee University, to speak to the troops. The
black soldiers who heard Dr. Moton "... reported that he
told them not to expect in the United States the kind of freedom they had enjoyed in France and that they must remain
content with the same position they had always occupied in
the United States. "[10]

Black people who remained at home during the war
were in store for a dramatic change in their lives. The
great migration between 1916 and 1918 was a movement moti-
vated by various political and economic conditions created by
the war efforts. These conditions made it attractive for black
people to migrate to the north. It is estimated that 300,000
blacks moved north during the peak migratory years, 1916 to
1918.

World War I also created dramatic changes in American industrial production. The northern industrialists experienced a business boom; the production of munitions and military goods for the allies increased the demand for unskilled
and semi-skilled laborers. The draft and the cessation of
European immigration created a severe labor shortage since
for years foreign immigration had constituted the chief source
of unskilled labor for northern industry.

There was a great need for unskilled workers in heavy
industry, and blacks in rural and urban areas of the South
were recruited. The employment of blacks as cheap labor
had always been an important part of the southern agricultural economy. During the war, northern industrialists actively pursued this cheap labor market.

[The] 3,000,000 Negroes engaged in agricultural
pursuits constituted in (1909) 30 percent of the rural
population of the south and 40 percent of all southern agricultural workers. Their skill and industry
govern, to a large degree, the prosperity of the
southern farmer.[11]

The plantation tenant system kept blacks under the
control of agricultural capitalists. Black landownership was
extremely hard to achieve. The black prospective buyer had
to be acceptable to the white community, acquire a white
sponsor, and was allowed to purchase only acreage that was
undesirable to whites. The independent black farmer was
rare;

... historically he has lacked enough cash to finance his operations, and so often sold himself
into debt at ruinous interest rates. He also lacked
enough land to diversify and so gambled heavily on
cotton. Over a span of some four decades, more
than half the black farm owners were squeezed off
the land.[12]

Below the independent landowners were the tenants
who did not own anything but their own labor. The black
tenant worked on a specified number of acres, and depending
upon the harvest, he was to receive a certain percentage of
the produce to feed his family and to sell on the open market. He had to do so under a very special set of rules.
Until recent times he was often required to make all his pur-
chases through the plantation commissary. If he lacked cash,
which was almost always, he was extended credit at exorbi-
tant interest. The debts were secured by a lien, which usually extended to anything the cropper owned and to all his
future produce.

If a tenant was so much in debt that he could never
pay the landlord off, the easiest way out was to move to another plantation. But,

... many a time he found himself having invested
a full season's work without having received anything near the wages he would have earned had he
been a wage laborer with full employment. On such
occasions at least, he had to face long months of
semi-starvation for himself and his family.[13]

Table III illustrates the class positions of blacks in the agricultural economy. Between 1910 and 1930 the percentage of black farm owners dropped 3.8 percent from 24.0 percent in 1910 to 20.2 percent in 1930. The largest contingent of black farm owners was in 1920, when 212,365 black people owned small farms.

TABLE III:

Number of Black Operators by Tenure and Sections

	Number of Farm Operators			Percent Distribution		
	1930	1920	1910	1930	1920	1910
Owners	176,130	313,365	211,087	20.2	32.2	24.0
Tenants	694,004	701,471	668,559	79.7	76.6	75.9
Managers	805	1,759	1,190	.1	.2	.1

Source: Negroes in the United States, 1920-1932, U.S. Department of Commerce, Bureau of Census, Government Printing Office, Washington, D.C.

The majority of blacks were tenant farmers. From 1910 to 1930, the black tenant farm population increased from 75.8 percent to 79.7 percent, a difference of 3.9 percent. Black tenant farmers reached a peak in population of 701,471 people in 1920. The smallest agricultural class among blacks was the farm manager. This class comprised 0.1 percent in 1930, 0.2 percent in 1920 and 0.1 percent in 1910. The black farmer was unable to compete with his white counterpart and usually his farming enterprise produced just enough to meet family needs and pay off debts. He could not garner enough profit to improve the farm or expand his production.

The farm manager kept watch over the field tenants and acted as a liaison between the black field hand and the plantation owner. The masses of blacks were tenant farmers, 79.7 percent of whom were unskilled. The tenants were locked in an agricultural economy that offered no opportunity for advancement and a decent way of life. The law of the

land was on the side of the landlord who could place liens
against his produce and sell the property of the tenant to meet
payment on any debts.

Along with economic deprivation, a natural disaster
occurred which precipitated mass migration. The Cotton Belt
of the South was struck first with drought and then heavy
rains; the boll weevil set upon the cotton crops.

> [As] a result, many of the farmers were almost
> ruined and many decided to change from cotton to
> food products. These food products were peanuts,
> corn, velvet beans, oats, sorghum and sweet po-
> tatoes which required only 70 to 80 percent of the
> labor which all-cotton crop requires.[14]

With the heavy rains, the invasion of the boll weevil,
and the new mechanizations developed to harvest peanuts,
corn, and sweet potatoes, many black tenants were unemployed, and the few independent black landowners were forced
to mechanize or go out of business.

The economic repression of blacks in the South was
fortified by political powerlessness and social segregation.
Politically, African-Americans were rendered powerless
through the literacy test, the poll tax, the grandfather clause,
and other unethical methods to keep blacks from voting and
exercising political power.

The social and economic factors for the great migration to the North were taking hold. Blacks were dispos-
sessed, unskilled workers in a changing agricultural economy.

In 1915 Henry Ford revolutionized American industry
by creating an eight-hour day and a five-dollar daily minimum
wage. Such work hours and wages were encouraging figures
for blacks who worked in the fields for hours earning as little as seventy-five cents per day or less.

Migration northward was assisted by Labor Agents
and the black press, which capitalized on the discontent to
offer appealing alternatives to the southern way of life.

Robert Abbott, editor and publisher of the Chicago
Defender, was the most vocal advocate of migration. The
paper editorialized the plight of southern blacks with headlines that played up the negative aspects of southern life

while exclaiming the virtues of northern living. Repeated sto-
ries of those who were leaving the South or who were already
in the North conveyed the excitement of a mass movement under way and created an atmosphere of religious hysteria.

The Defender was helped a great deal by "negroes
already in the north writing letters to relatives and friends in
the south. Such letters were often passed on by word of
mouth among the illiterates."[15]

Labor agents, backed by northern industrial concerns,
were instrumental in recruiting as much as 20 percent of the
black workers who migrated.

There were many cases of mass transport. Steel
mills and railroads sent special trains to the South to transport workers to the North. The fee and expenses for the
transportation by rail was charged against the worker's future
wages.

Table IV (on page 36) illustrates the rapid increase
of black residents in thirteen major northern cities. All of
these urban centers experienced dramatic population changes.
For example, New York City in 1910 had a total of 91,709
black residents; by 1920, 152,467 blacks resided in New York
City, an increase of 60,758 people, or 66.3 percent. Chicago, Illinois, in 1910 had a black population of 44,103; ten
years later 109,458 blacks lived in Chicago, an astronomical
increase of 148.2 percent. Detroit, Michigan, the hub of the
automobile industry in 1910, had a black population of only
5,471. By 1920 there were 40,838 black residents in Detroit.
Black migration to the North was an attempt to acquire better
occupational opportunities in the war-inflated economy.

Black industrial employment during World War I was
concentrated in a few fields. Blacks were iron and steel
workers, meat packers, shipbuilders and automobile workers.
There were always positions open in the "traditional" black
occupations as domestics, maintenance men, and road construc-
tion workers. Racist hiring practices, labor unions, and re-
sentful white workers effectively retarded black workers' opportunities. Owners "of northern industry were not very willing to hire negro workers except when orders were piling up,
and European immigrant laborers could not be had because of
the war or legal restrictions on immigration."[16]

Employment statistics show a steady increase in black
employment, but blacks dominated only three areas--agricul-

TABLE IV:

Cities Having A Black Population Of 19,000 Or More In 1930 With Comparative Figures For 1920 And 1910

City	1930	1920	1910	1920-1930 Number	1920-1930 Percent	1910-1920 Number	1910-1920 Percent
New York, N. Y.	327,706	152,467	91,709	175,239	114.9%	60,758	66.3%
Chicago, Ill.	233,903	109,458	44,103	124,445	113.7%	65,355	148.2%
Philadephia, Pa.	219,599	134,229	84,459	85,370	63.3%	49,770	58.9%
Baltimore, Md.	142,106	108,322	84,749	33,784	31.2%	23,573	27.8%
Washington, D. C.	132,068	109,966	94,446	22,102	20.1%	15,520	16.4%
Detroit, Mich.	120,066	40,838	5,741	79,228	194.0%	35,097	611.3%
St. Louis, Mo.	93,580	69,854	43,960	23,726	34.0%	25,894	58.9%
Cleveland, Ohio	71,899	34,451	8,448	37,448	108.7%	26,003	307.8%
Pittsburgh, Pa.	47,818	30,079	19,639	17,739	59.0%	10,440	53.2%
Newark, N. J.	38,880	16,977	9,475	21,903	129.0%	7,502	79.2%
Boston, Mass.	20,514	16,350	13,564	4,225	25.8%	2,786	20.5%
East St. Louis, Ill.	11,536	7,437	5,882	4,099	55.1%	1,555	26.4%

Source: Negroes in the United States, 1920-1932, Bureau of the Census, U.S. Government Printing Office, 1935.

ture, domestic and personal service, and high rates of employment in the manufacturing and mechanical industries.
These three occupations employed 89 percent of the black population in 1910: agriculture, 54.8 percent; manufacturing and mechanical industries, 12.6 percent; domestic and personal service, 21.6 percent.   In 1920 the same three occupations employed 84.9 percent of the black population: agriculture, 44.2 percent; manufacturing and mechanical industries, 18.7 percent; and domestic services, 22.0 percent.   In 1930 these occupations employed 83.3 percent: agriculture, 36.1 percent; manufacturing and mechanical industries, 18.6 percent; and domestic and personal service, 28.6 percent. *

These figures reveal that there was some advancement during this period but there was no upward mobility.   Blacks were hired in "traditional black jobs" as field hands and sharecroppers in agriculture and as maids, butlers, and servants in domestic services.   The manufacturing and mechanical industries were the highest employer of blacks in "non-traditional" jobs.

On November 11, 1918, World War I ended and many able-bodies black and white men returned to the United States industrial centers seeking employment.   The influx of service men to the job market caused much unemployment among blacks once more.

The economic inequality blacks were suffering in northern industry was augmented by segregated housing conditions which made the new black community a municipal problem for many urban centers.   The manufacturing and railroad interest which spearheaded the transportation of blacks to the North ignored the social welfare of the men.   "They saw them crowded into wretched cabins, without water or any of the conveniences of life, their wives and children condemned to live in the disreputable quarters of the town and made no effort to lift them out of the mire."[17]

Soon the industrial centers became crowded and blacks moved into previously all-white districts: competition and the diminishing job market brought blacks and whites into violent conflicts.   There were approximately eighteen major interracial disturbances between 1915 and 1919.

---

* Negroes in the United States, 1920-1932, Bureau of the Census, U.S. Government Printing Office, 1935.

Toward the end of World War I interracial violence
had spread throughout America. Such headlines as "Race Riot
in East St. Louis," "Nine Killed in Chicago," and "Riot in
Nation's Capital" were frequent in newspapers during this period. The social conditions " ... needed for a 'race war' were
created on whites while relegating blacks to a subordinate position. "[18]

When the Depression began in 1929, millions of Americans were not capable of supporting themselves and needed
relief payments. By 1934, 17 percent of whites and 38 percent of blacks were incapable of self-support. The Depression
pushed millions out of work; the relief rolls and the bread
lines grew longer. The Depression added to the distress of
blacks seeking freedom from want; " ... added to denials of
freedom and democracy was the specter of starvation. "[19]

Conditions of American society between 1914 and 1930
changed the character of the black population. The social
changes transformed a large segment of the black population
from rural farmhands to urban workers.

Such major urban centers as Detroit, Cleveland, Philadelphia, Newark, Chicago, and New York City experienced
rapid increases of their black population. Housing conditions,
as previously discussed, coupled with competition with whites
for jobs, touched off racial violence throughout the United
States.

These social conditions made black nationalism an attractive alternative for African-Americans. The Nation of Islam began in the black community of Detroit in 1930 during an
era of hunger, discontent, anguish, and disillusionment. "So
it was that in Detroit there appeared in the black ghetto a mys-
terious messiah called W. D. Fard Muhammad. His mission
was to wake the dead Nation in the West. "[20]

Chapter III will investigate the origin and development
of the Nation of Islam's ideology and leadership. The chapter
will also analyze the relationship between the Nation of Islam
and the Moorish Science Temple.

NOTES

1. Arthur E. Barbeau and Henry Florette, The Unknown
Soldiers (Philadelphia: Temple University Press, 1974), p. 37.

2. Jack D. Foner, Blacks and the Military in American History (New York: Praeger Publishers, 1974), p. 112.

3. Emmett J. Scott, "The Participation of Negroes in World War I," Journal of Negro Education XII, (Summer 1943), p. 35.

4. Barbeau and Florette, Unknown Soldiers, p. 44.

5. Historical Section, Army War College, Order of Battle of the United States Land Forces in the World War (Washington, D.C.: Government Printing Office, 1931), p. 431.

6. Emmett J. Scott, Scott's Official History of the American Negro in the World War (Chicago: L.W. Walters, 1919), p. 82.

7. Foner, Blacks and the Military, p. 123.

8. Ulysses Lee, The Employment of Negro Troops U.S. Army in World War II (Washington, D.C.: U.S. Army, 1966), p. 10.

9. W.E.B. DuBois, "An Essay Toward a History of the Black Man in the Great War," The Crisis, Vol. 18 (May-October 1919), p. 70.

10. John H. Franklin, From Slavery to Freedom (New York: Random House, 1969), p. 469.

11. U.S. Bureau of Education, Negro Education in the United States (Washington, D.C.: U.S. Printing Office, 1917), p. 73.

12. George W. Groh, The Black Migration (New York: Weybright & Talley, 1972), p. 32.

13. Gunnar Myrdal, An American Dilemma (New York: Harper and Brothers, 1944), p. 246.

14. Thomas J. Woofter, Negro Migration (New York: Negro Universities Press, 1969), p. 79.

15. Myrdal, American Dilemma, p. 194.

16. Ibid., p. 195.

17.   Allen Grimshaw, Racial Violence in the United
States (Chicago: Aldine, 1969), p. 63.

18.   Paul Mitchell, ed., Race Riots in Black and
White (Englewood Cliffs, N.J.:   Prentice-Hall, 1970), p. 1-2.

19.   Franklin, From Slavery, p. 496.

20.   Eric C. Lincoln, The Black Muslims in America (Canada: Saunders of Toronto, 1961), p. xxv.

Chapter III

THE MOORISH SCIENCE TEMPLE

> "Fard Muhammad studied Noble Drew Ali's ap-
> proach to introduce the Koran to the black com-
> munity. Professor Fard introduced the whole
> text of the Koran, in the very inception of the
> Nation of Islam. To introduce it he had to put
> it in the package of Drew Ali."
> > --Imam Wallace D. Muhammad
> > Chief Minister, World Com-
> > munity of Al-Islam in the West

Social conditions after the Depression left Americans in general and the African-American community in particular in a
state of disorganization. High unemployment, low wages, discrimination in housing and the treatment black servicemen received after World War I created discontent among African-
Americans. These social and economic factors made it conducive for a black nationalist movement to emerge as a vehicle for social reform.

The Nation of Islam evolved from the Moorish Science
Organization, founded by Timothy Drew, who was born in
North Carolina in 1886. (See Table V on page 42). Drew
was a semi-literate migrant to Newark, New Jersey, who
worked as a train expressman before starting the first Moorish Science Temple there in 1913.

Drew came upon two revelations which radically influenced his thinking. "He encountered some forms of Oriental
philosophy and was impressed with its racial catholicity."[1]
According to the legend of the movement, Timothy Drew made
a pilgrimage to North Africa" ... where he received a com-

TABLE V

Evolution Of The Moorish Science Temple
And The Nation Of Islam

Moorish-American
Science Temple

(Newark 1913)

NOBLE DREW ALI
(B. Timothy Drew)

Drew Ali dies (1929)

JOHN GIVENS EL and W. D. FARD

(each claims to be reincarnation of
Noble Drew Ali)

Moors remain faithful to:

JOHN GIVENS EL   W. D. FARD

(Chicago 1930)   (Detroit 1930)

Fard disappears (1933)

Two factions developed:

Fard as prophet,   Fard as Allah,

ABDUL MUHAMMAD   ELIJAH MUHAMMAD
                                  establishes headquarters
                                  in Chicago

                                  Nation of Islam

mission from the King of Morocco to teach Islam to the Negroes in the United States."[2]   Drew had to pass a test to
prove he was the prophet of Allah.   The test involved the
pyramids of Egypt, in which Drew was allegedly released inside and had to find his way out.   Drew " ... mastered the
pyramids and they knew he was the prophet; he came back to
the Temple in New Jersey in 1913."[3]

Timothy Drew changed his name to Noble Drew Ali and
began to spread his doctrine in basements, empty lots, and
street corners of Newark, New Jersey.   Noble Drew Ali had
very little formal education, but " ... a certain magnetic
charm, a sincerity of purpose and a real determination to
lead his people out of the difficulties of racial prejudice and
discrimination brought him followers."[4]

NATIONALITY

Marcus Garvey's Universal Negro Improvement Association
(UNIA) and Drew Ali's Moorish Science Temple flourished
about the same time, though Garvey had many more followers
than Ali.   Garvey started the UNIA in Jamaica 1914 and founded a branch in Harlem in 1916.

Members of the Moorish Science Temple believe that
Marcus Garvey " ... was a forerunner to plant the seed in the
people and prepare them to be received by Noble Drew Ali."[5]
Unlike Garvey, however, Drew Ali did not call for emigration
to Africa.   Drew Ali's nationalism was purely psychological.

Noble Drew Ali and his followers" ... sought a psychic
escape by changing their names and the symbols of their culture; [they] hoped to change their social fortunes."[6]   Drew
Ali advocated that true emancipation would come through knowledge of black Americans' African heritage and by becoming
Muslims.   He also felt that Christianity was for Europeans
and Islam was for people of African descent.   Peace on earth
was not possible, according to Ali, until each racial group
has its own "true religion."

Noble Drew Ali advocated that individuals must know
themselves and their nationality before they can know Allah.
Drew Ali founded the Moorish Science Temple upon the idea
that African-Americans are Asiatics, specifically Moors, whose
ancestors had come from Morocco.   Moorish Americans are
" ... descendants of the ancient Moabites who inhabited the

northwestern and southwestern shores of Africa. "[7] Drew Ali
also taught his members to believe that when a star and crescent moon were seen in the sky, "this betokened the arrival
of the day of the Asiatics and the destruction of the Europeans. "[8]

Noble Drew Ali's doctrine inspired Fard Muhammad to
create similar value systems for the Nation of Islam. (See
Table VI on page 45). During an interview with Imam Wallace D. Muhammad, he explained how Fard Muhammad taught
members of the Nation of Islam that "We were Black Asiatics
and that's what Drew Ali taught his people. Fard taught us
we were descendants from a great Islamic Kingdom and Drew
Ali taught his people the same. "[9] Drew Ali taught that people of African descent were subjugated to white domination because they used names like colored, black, or Ethiopian.

Noble Drew Ali provided African-Americans " ... with
a new national origin that made them part of a far-flung Moorish nation that had somehow made its way to North America. "[10]

Noble Drew Ali's philosophy was published in his 64-
page Holy Koran, a pamphlet consisting of principles from the
Islamic Koran, the Christian Bible, some of Marcus Garvey's
African nationalist ideas, and Drew Ali's own historical interpretations. The Holy Koran is regarded as a book to be read
only by his followers.

The Holy Koran proclaimed that Noble Drew Ali was a
prophet, ordained by Allah to carry the message of Islam to
people of African descent in America. Membership in Ali's
Moorish Science Temple was restricted to Asiatics only, by
which he meant any person who is non-Caucasian. Moorish
Americans, however, were overwhelmingly comprised of black
people.

RITUALS AND PRACTICES

When attending services in the temple men and women are
segregated. At all times male members wear a red fez with
a black tassle. Men are allowed to wear beards, and when
not attending official functions they may dress casually. The
fruit of Islam's uniforms in the Nation of Islam are fashioned
after the Moorish Americans, "the dress Fard Muhammad
originally gave male members of the Fruit of Islam is the
same dress Drew Ali's people had. "[11] Moorish-American

TABLE VI

Organizational Comparisons Between
Moorish Science Temple And Nation Of Islam

	Moorish Science Temple	Nation of Islam
Nationality	Moorish Americans	Asiatic-Black
Prophet	Noble Drew Ali	Elijah Muhammad
Religion	Islam	Islam
Land	No desire for separate state, psychological separation through Moorish status	Separate state
Sacred text	Koran created by Noble Drew Ali	Islamic Koran and Christian Bible
God	Allah	Allah in the form of Fard Muhammad
Race	Asiatics	Asiatic Blacks (Tribe of Shabazz)
Place of Worship	Temple	Mosque
Heaven	In the mind	On earth
Separation of Sexes	Yes	Yes
Names	Bey, El	X--Replace slave name because real name unknown
Dress	Men--Fez worn during official functions, beards and mustaches allowed, suit and tie optional Women--Turbans optional, no make-up, pants, long dresses to shoe tops	Men--Suit and ties, clean shaven Women--Head covered, no make-up, long dresses to shoe tops
Citizenship	United States of America	Nation of Islam, Nation within a Nation

marriages are monogamous and divorce is rarely permitted.
In most cases the husband is the only source of financial support and women are expected to be housewives.

Women wear pants or long dresses and no make-up.
A turban is worn only with long dresses. It is not considered
appropriate to wear pants with the turban. On Fridays (their
Sabbath) women must wear long white dresses which fall below the knee when seated. On Sunday and Wednesday night
meetings (8:00-10:00 p.m.), they are free to dress as they
please, but they should never wear revealing clothes. Sunday
School is conducted for children from 5 p.m. to 7 p.m.

Moorish Americans pray three times daily--at sunrise,
noon, and sunset. When praying, members stand facing the
east toward Mecca. They use two words of greeting, "peace"
and "Islam" with the right hand raised and palm out. Moorish Americans attach special significance to their dress, especially the fez and turban. They believe the "fez is the first
head dress worn by man and the turban the first head dress
worn by woman. The fez and turban symbolize that knowledge is embedded within them and these wraps protect the
wearer."[12] Moorish Americans also adhere to a strict veg-
etarian diet. No meat or eggs are to be eaten, but fish and
vegetables are prescribed. Smoking, drinking liquor, straight-
ening the hair, and using cosmetics are forbidden. Sports
and games, attendance at motion pictures, and secular danc-
ing are also discouraged.

Drew Ali created a Moorish flag which is red with a
green five-pointed star in the center. The points on the star
represent truth, love, peace, justice, and freedom. The
Moorish flag is usually next to the American flag in all meetings. Moorish Americans are "loyal citizens of the United
States and pledge allegiance to its flag."[13]

ORGANIZATION

The Temple is the main organizational unit of the Moorish
Science Movement. The national headquarters, located in
Chicago, originally had a membership of 10,000. Drew Ali
established temples in Detroit, Harlem, Pittsburgh, Philadelphia, Kansas City, West Virginia, Brooklyn, Richmond (Virginia), South Carolina, and Augusta (Georgia). Overall membership was approximately 30,000. Financial support for the
organization is derived from dues collected at the various tem-

ples and numerous businesses.   Leaders of the temples are
called grand sheiks.   Beneath the sheiks are ministers, eld-
ers, and stewards.   Rank and file members are referred to
as brothers and sisters.   All Moorish Americans must attach
the term "El" or "Bey" to their names.

FREE NATIONAL NAME

To become a member of the Moorish Science Temple individuals must affirm their desire to follow Noble Drew Ali and
pay an initiation fee of $1.00.   New members are given a
free national name and a nationality card.

Moorish Americans refer to the El or Bey as their
"free national name."   The national name represents " ...
African heritage which allows you to be a citizen in the international affair.   In the affairs of nations those people not of
a nation receive no consideration."[14]   Moorish Americans are
required to carry a nationality card which bears the following
inscription:

(Replica of Star and Crescent)	UNITY (Replica of Clasped Hands)	(Replica of Circle "7")

MEMBER'S NAME

_____

This is your nationality and identification card
for the Moorish Science Temple of America,
and birthright for the Moorish-Americans.   We
honor all the divine prophets, Jesus, Mohammad,
Buddha and Confucius.   May the blessings of
God of our father Allah, be upon you that carry this card.   I do hereby declare that you are
a Muslim under the Divine Law of the Holy Koran of Mecca--Love, Truth, Peace, Freedom
and Justice.   "I am a citizen of the USA."
             Noble Drew Ali, The Prophet
             3810 Wabash Avenue
             Chicago, Illinois

Moorish Americans believed the sight of the nationality

card would stop individual and institutional oppression by white
Americans. Members of the Moorish Science Temple began
accosting " ... the white enemy on the streets, showing their
membership card and buttons, and proclaiming in the name of
their prophet, Noble Drew Ali, that they had been freed of
European domination."[15] Soon after these altercations Drew
Ali ordered his followers to stop " ... flashing your cards at
Europeans."

NOBLE DREW ALI REINCARNATED

In 1929 Drew Ali began to designate more power to his subordinates. His subordinates began to exploit the members by
selling herbs, magic charms, and literature on the movement
to the extent that some of them became wealthy. Drew Ali
attempted to stop this dishonest practice and became a pawn
in the struggle for power.

One of his sheiks, Claude Greene, a former butler of
philanthropist, Julius Rosenwald, challenged Drew Ali's leadership. Current members of the Moorish Science Temple advocate that Sheik Claude Greene was a minor character in the
splintering of the organization. Noble Drew Ali was reputed
to have taught four men and instructed them to carry out his
mission. Elijah Muhammad was one of them. "Daddy Grace,
Father Divine and Carlos Cookman, none of them did what
Noble Drew Ali asked them to. All they wanted was that gold
for themselves."[16]

During the conflict between the factions Sheik Claude
Greene was shot to death on March 15, 1929, in his office at
the Unity Club. Drew Ali was not in Chicago at the time;
nevertheless, he was arrested and charged with the murder.
Drew Ali was released on bond and died a few weeks later.

All theories of his death point to two circumstances.
He either died from injuries inflicted by police during his
imprisonment or was killed by followers loyal to Sheik Claude
Greene.

The story of Noble Drew Ali's death is told differently
by members of the Moorish Science Temple. George Bey, a
Moorish American for 25 years and minister of Temple #7 in
Richmond, Virginia, said, " ... his health went bad on him;
as far as I know he died a natural death."[17]

When Drew Ali died and Marcus Garvey was deported, there was a severe leadership crisis within the black nationalist movement. Two men, Wali Fard Muhammad and John Givens El, attempted to solve the problem by claiming to be Noble Drew Ali reincarnated.

John Givens El was Noble Drew Ali's chauffeur. It is reputed that while he was working on Drew Ali's automobile, shortly after Ali's death, he fainted. John Givens El's eyes were examined; "He had the sign of the star and crescent in his eyes and they knew right then he was the prophet reincarnated into his chauffeur."[18]

Those who believed John Givens El are the present day Moorish Americans. Those who believed W. Fard Muhammad's reincarnation comprised what came to be known as the Nation of Islam.

The following chapter is a discussion of the Nation of Islam's doctrine under the leadership of Wali Fard and Chief Assistant, Elijah Muhammad.

NOTES

1. Arthur F. Fauset, Black Gods of the Metropolis (Philadelphia: University of Pennsylvania Press, 1944), p. 41.

2. E. U. Essien-Udom, Black Nationalism: A Search for an Identity in America (Chicago: University of Chicago Press, 1962), p. 34.

3. Interview, Sam Bey, Member of Moorish Science Temple, Richmond, Virginia, August 4, 1976.

4. Fauset, Black Gods, p. 42.

5. Interview, Minister George Bey of Moorish Science Temple, Richmond, Virginia, August 4, 1976.

6. Eric C. Lincoln, The Black Muslims in America (Canada: Saunders of Toronto, 1961), p. 52.

7. Drew Ali, The Holy Koran of the Moorish Holy Temple of Science (Chicago: privately published, n.d.).

8. Fauset, Black Gods, p. 42.

9. Interview, Imam Wallace D. Muhammad, Chicago, Illinois, July 25, 1979.

10. Theodore Draper, The Rediscovery of Black Nationalism (New York: Viking Press, 1969), p. 70-71.

11. Interview, Imam Wallace D. Muhammad.

12. Interview, Frank Bey, Moorish Science Temple, August 4, 1976.

13. Draper, Rediscovery, p. 71.

14. Interview, Bill El, Moorish Science Temple, August 4, 1976.

15. Arna Bontemps and Jack Conroy, They Seek a City (New York: Doubleday, 1945), p. 176.

16. Interview, Minister George Bey.

17. Ibid.

18. Interview, Sam Bey, November 12, 1975.

Chapter IV

THE NATION OF ISLAM

> "The Nation of Islam was a religion and a so-
> cial movement organization. In fact, the reli-
> gion as it was introduced to the membership
> was more a social reform philosophy than Or-
> thodox Islam."
>
> --Imam Wallace D. Muham-
> mad, Chief Minister, WCIW

During the summer of 1930, W. Fard Muhammad, often referred to as professor Fard or Wali, appeared in the Paradise Valley Community of Detroit, Michigan, claiming to be
Noble Drew Ali reincarnated. Fard's mission was to gain
freedom, justice, and equality for people of African descent
residing in the United States. Fard proclaimed himself the
leader of the Nation of Islam with remedies to cure problems
in the African-American community: " ... social problems,
lack of economic development, undisciplined family life and
alcoholism."[1]

Fard claimed he was born in Mecca on February 26,
1877. His light color and Oriental features fostered the belief that he was an Arab. Fard maintained he was of royal
ancestry," ... the son of a wealthy member of the tribe of
Kareish to which the prophet Muhammad belonged."[2] Fard
was reputed to have received an education at the University
of California and spent several years studying in England to
" ... be trained for a diplomatic career in the service of the
Kingdom of Hejaz."[3]

Wali Fard earned a living as a street peddler. He

pushed a cart along the streets selling silks and artifacts door
to door.   Fard claimed the silks and clothing were like the
garb worn by blacks in their original homeland, Africa.   When
Fard gained access to people's homes, he discussed three
concepts which became the foundation of his ideology: "Allah
is God, the white man is the devil and the so-called Negroes
are the Asiatic Black people, the cream of the planet earth. "[4]

Fard taught from the Bible until he introduced the Koran to his membership.   Fard published two documents containing his doctrine, Teachings for the Lost-Found Nation in
a Mathematical Way and Secret Ritual of the Nation of Islam,
which were orally transmitted.   Freedom, justice, and equality could not be achieved in the United States, Fard felt, until
blacks regained their true religion (Islam), their language
(Arabic), and a separate autonomous state.

Gradually Fard Muhammad introduced himself to his
followers as a " ... Christ figure to displace the old Christ
that Christianity gave black people. "[5]   Fard was accepted as
a Christ figure because he convinced his followers " ... that
Christianity is geared toward the enslavement of the individual's mind.   It demands the imagination of a child to accept
something unseen and immaterial. "[6]

To reinforce his Christ image Fard often mesmerized
his followers with feats of magic.   Once, members placed
strands of their hair in a pile and Fard took a strand of hair
from his head and with it lifted all of them up.   Followers
interpreted this to mean "Lift me up and I will draw all men
unto me. "[7]   Often Fard would attend sermons and his hair
would be completely gray; " ... he would appear the next time
and [have] no gray hair.   He made it a purpose to draw their
attention to that. "[8]

Fard perceived Christianity as the white man's religion,
one that didn't offer solutions to social problems or development of the "Asiatic Nation. "   Members of the Nation of Islam also believe that white people are inherently evil and,
therefore, it is not in their nature to accept Islam and become
Muslims.   However, Islam is the nature of black people.
Wali Fard also perceived a "natural" conflict between Islam
and Christianity.   This conflict would ultimately be resolved
through the Battle of Armageddon, which he defined as a religious war between Muslims and Christians.

Fard began to arrange more meetings in private homes

and gathered a small devoted group of followers. The former peddler assumed the role of the prophet. Membership at the house meetings became so large that his followers rented a hall which they called their temple. At that point the Nation of Islam was born.

Between 1930 and 1933, Fard recruited 8,000 followers among Detroit blacks. The rapid growth of Fard's organization made it necessary for Fard to train several ministers to help manage the organization's affairs. One of the first ministers was an unemployed auto worker named Elijah Poole.

Elijah Poole was born in Sandersville, Georgia, on October 7, 1898. His father, Wali Poole, was a Baptist minister and a sharecropper who supported a wife and thirteen children. Elijah attended public schools in Georgia. Poole " ... learned only the bare rudiments of reading, writing and arithmetic before he had to go to the fields to help his family earn a living."[9]

Elijah Poole worked in Sandersville and in Macon, Georgia, as a laborer for the Southern Railroad. Later he was employed as a builder for the Cherokee Brick Company and was appointed foreman in 1919. While Poole was employed in Macon, he met and married Clara Evans. In 1923, Elijah, Clara, and their two sons (Emmanuel and Nathaniel) moved to Detroit. The Poole family increased to four more sons (Herbert, Elijah II, Wallace, Akbar) and two daughters (Ethel and Lotta). Elijah Poole worked for the Chevrolet Auto Plant in Detroit from 1923 to 1929. The Depression caused the family to go on relief for two years, from 1929 to 1931.

One night in 1931, Elijah Poole attended one of Wali Fard's sermons. While talking to Fard after the meeting, Poole said, "I know who you are, you're God himself." Fard whispered to Poole, "That's right, but don't tell it now. It is not yet time for me to be known."[10]

Shortly after Poole encountered Fard, he began to study Islam. Elijah Poole became a minister and was given the name Kariem and eventually adopted the name Elijah Muhammad. Elijah Muhammad was so devoted to Fard that he was named the Chief Minister of Islam and became Fard's eventual successor.

Elijah Muhammad was the son of a Baptist minister;

that is one reason why " ... Fard Muhammad chose him because he was so learned in the Bible.   The people were already Bible-oriented. "[11]

       In 1932 Elijah Muhammad moved to Chicago where he
established Temple #2.   He returned to Detroit to aid Fard,
who had been imprisoned that year.   Released and ordered
out of Detroit on May 26, 1933, Fard went to Temple #2 in
Chicago and was arrested again.   After a series of police
confrontations, Fard gradually withdrew from the organization.
When Fard left, Elijah Muhammad taught his followers that
Fard was God in person.   Fard's absence fortified the belief
that he was God momentarily assuming a human form to alleviate the oppression suffered by African-Americans.   Elijah
Muhammad was almost " ... singlehandedly responsible for
the deification of Fard and for the perpetuation of his teachings in the early years after Fard disappeared. "[12]   One of
the ministers of the organization, Abdul Muhammad, organized a group of Muslims loyal to the Constitution of the United
States.   A different faction which believed Fard was Allah,
established an organization in Chicago in 1934 under the guidance of Elijah Muhammad.   The Detroit Temple eventually
became a branch of Elijah Muhammad's organization.

       Temple #2 became the main headquarters for the Na-
tion of Islam after Fard's disappearance.   Temple #2 in Chicago was located at 5335 South Greenwood Avenue and adjacent
to it is the University of Islam at 5333 South Greenwood Avenue.   In his role as messenger of Allah, Elijah Muhammad
became the master architect to develop the ideology started
by Wali Fard.

       Elijah Muhammad ran his organization as the absolute
authority.   Muhammad appointed ministers of each temple; he
also appointed supreme captains who were responsible to him.
Beneath the supreme captains were captains, then first, second and third lieutenants.   The Temples were not autonomous;
all orders had to be cleared through Elijah Muhammad.

                            NATIONALITY

Individuals interested in becoming members of the Nation of
Islam were required to send the following letter to the Chicago headquarters:

       Mr. E. Muhammad
       4847 So. Woodlawn Avenue

Chicago 15, Illinois

Dear Mr. Muhammad:

I have been attending the teachings of Islam by one of your Ministers. I believe in
It, and I bear witness that there is no God
But Allah and that Muhammad is Thy Servant
and Apostle. I desire to reclaim my Own.
Please give me my Original name. My slave
name is as follows:

Name

Address

City and State

After forwarding this letter the prospective member
was required to answer several questions concerning marital
status, number of children, and age. When this procedure
was completed individuals were assigned their X. The Nation
of Islam requires members to change their last names to X
in order to rid themselves of their "slave names." The X
also stands for the unknown identity associated with the African ancestry. Each member of a Temple is assigned an X.
If there are two people with the same first name, a number
is attached to the X. For example, if James X is a member
of Temple #2 and James Smith becomes a Muslim and also
joins Temple #2, he is designated James 1X.

Members of the Nation of Islam referred to their nationality as Asiatics, " ... descendants of the original black
nation of Asia, of the Great Asiatic nation, from the continent
of Africa. "[13]

Within the Asiatic nation is a group known as the "Tribe
of Shabazz," which they believed originated in Africa when a
great explosion divided the earth from the moon some 60 tril-
lion years ago. The Tribe of Shabazz discovered " ... the
best part of our planet to live on, the rich Nile Valley of
Egypt and the present seat of the Holy City, Mecca."[14] Elijah Muhammad's Tribe of Shabazz is an attempt to equip black
Americans with an African identity. The Nation of Islam
helped the membership to believe, " ... at least in fantasy,
the glorious history of Black Afro-Asia. "[15]

The Tribe of Shabazz (people of African descent) were enslaved for four hundred years. African-Americans constitute the Nation of Islam. Wali Fard and his messenger Elijah Muhammad were sent to relocate the "lost-found nation" in an independent state.

Elijah Muhammad renounced his citizenship and urged his followers to do the same. Muhammad taught that "We (so-called Negroes) are not and cannot be American citizens, since we are not American by nature or race."[16]

THE DEVIL

The "white man is the devil" theme propagated by the Nation of Islam was a direct inspiration from the teachings of Noble Drew Ali. Drew Ali " ... identified white people with the embodiment of evil in Scripture, which is Satan."[17]

Drew Ali interpreted the Bible to define whites " ... as the rider on the pale horse," which was a symbol of death. He " ... took that out of the Bible to identify the white man as the pale horse, whose rider is death."[18] Fard Muhammad was a student of comparative religious studies. He was able to detect " ... what the average follower of Drew Ali couldn't. The Caucasian race is the embodiment of evil. Fard came out in plain language and said they are devils."[19]

Part of the Muslim doctrine created the Tribe of Shabazz; another segment introduced an elaborate mythology which depicted the "devil" as white people. The doctrine describes a scientist named Yacub, who was a descendant of the Tribe of Shabazz 6800 years ago in the Holy City of Mecca. Yacub ran into conflict with Meccan authorities and was exiled with 59,999 of his followers to an island called Patmos in the Aegean Sea. There Yacub created a vengeful plot to enslave the Tribe of Shabazz. Yacub was skilled in genetics and through cross-breeding, he supposedly developed the white race.

It took Yacub several stages to create whites out of the black race. First he created the brown; 200 years later he created the red race from brown. It took 200 more years to create the yellow race from the red, and 6000 years ago he created the white race out of the yellow.

The first white person Yacub created was Adam and soon Eve followed. Adam's descendants, " ... at first walk-

ing on all fours and living in caves and trees (also mating
with beast) stayed on Patmos for six hundred years before
they escaped to the mainland. "[20]

After two thousand years, Allah raised up Moses to
civilize the white race, but even Moses found his task difficult. Yacub's white race was destined to rule for six thousand years until 1914.

SEPARATISM

Members of the Nation of Islam believed that their organization was a black nation within the United States and that Muslims were citizens of Mecca who saluted the Islamic flag.

Muslims believed African-Americans must free themselves physically (a separate state) and psychologically (Asiatics). Separation " ... can take a psychological, a religious
and an economic form even if it cannot express itself in the
ultimate guise of a national territory. "[21]

Vertical (upward) mobility in the United States' system
is limited by institutional racism and economic inequality.
Elijah Muhammad felt the solution was not integration into the
system, but separation. Charles 4X Jackson, a Muslim, compared Elijah Muhammad to Moses. He said, "Elijah is Moses, he is the one saying 'Pharaoh, let my people go.' He's
saying, 'Let's separate, we want to leave the White man. "[22]

The program of the Nation of Islam made an appeal
for a separate state, but if a separate state was not obtained,
they demanded equal employment opportunity and justice for
African-Americans.

Elijah Muhammad advocated, "We have as much right
to the soil as the white man. Why should we claim the land
of our Black brother in Africa; our destiny is right here in
America. "[23] Elijah Muhammad explained his position as
follows:

> We want to establish a separate state or territory
> to ourselves in this country or elsewhere. Our for-
> mer slave masters are obligated to maintain, to
> supply our needs in this zone or territory for the
> next twenty-five years, until we are able to produce
> and supply our own needs. "[24]

A separate state within the United States is a fantasy.
For internal security reasons the government would not allow
it, a reality Elijah Muhammad himself was aware of. Elijah
Muhammad admitted, "They will never give us three or four
states. That I probably know, but that doesn't hinder you and
me from asking for it."[25]

SELF-HELP

Elijah Muhammad's economic program is an attempt to encourage self-help through collective ownership of business.
Members must adhere to a strict moral and economic code
which will foster thrift, capital gain, independence and self-
respect. Muslims pray five times a day, eat once a day, and
abstain from pork, alcohol, tobacco, narcotics, gambling,
sports, long vacations from work, and sleeping more than is
necessary for health.

Each individual within the organization is responsible
for his or her own behavior and must assist others in adhering to the code of ethics. "Doing your own thing" is not permitted. Sharon Shabazz, a Muslim official, says lack of discipline is " ... destroying the moral fiber of the whole country. Alcohol, smoking whether it's dope or cigarettes, it
destroys the moral standard, the physical being and the society."[26]

Muslims advocate complete economic independence from
white America. But until they achieve a "state," their economic survival depends on the establishment of a black business industry which provides jobs for members and consumable
supplies and services to the community. Muslims are encouraged to pool their resources and invest in the black business.

To accomplish economic security for the Nation of Islam, Elijah Muhammad created an "Economic Blueprint" which
consists of five propositions:

1. Recognize the necessity for unity and group operation (activities).

2. Pool your resources, physically as well as financially.

3. Stop wanton criticism, of everything that is black-
   owned and black-operated.

    4.   Keep in mind--jealousy destroys from within.

    5.   Work hard in a collective manner.[27]

       Muslims also regularly give part of their income to the Nation of Islam. These contributions are given as "alms" (for the "cause of Islam"). The author has attended several meetings and witnessed a literal competition between members giving what they could afford. From the highest bill to the smallest copper coin, each cent which was donated to the cause received a loud "Praise Allah!"

THE UNIVERSITY OF ISLAM

Established in the 1930's by Elijah Muhammad, the University of Islam provided schooling for students in grades 4 through 12. During its first years of operation, the Detroit Board of Education attempted to close the University of Islam and return the students to public schools. Several Muslim teachers, including Elijah Muhammad, were arrested for contributing to the delinquency of minors. The court released the Muslims and suspended the sentences.

       Currently the institution is known as Clara Muhammad School. The curriculum includes African and African-American history, language skills, math, science and Islamic relations. Observance of dietary laws is encouraged and there is a Parent-Teacher Association. Muslim children go to school fifty weeks a year with no vacation (except for holidays Muslims observe). There is no sport or play; rest, snack, and free periods are eliminated.

       The girls, clad in long dresses, their heads mostly covered by scarves, attend school in the morning from 8:00 to 11:00 a.m. They are taught the same academic subjects as boys. To supplement their formal education, they attend the "Muslim Girls in Training" course (MGT), which teaches basic domestic skills-housekeeping, child-rearing, and hygiene.

       There is a junior MGT for young women between the ages of 15 and 19. Originally the 15- to 19-year-old group was called the General Civilization Class. Women in the organization were required to adhere to the following rules, referred to as "Laws of Islam":

    1.   Do not use lipstick or make-up.

2. Do not wear hair up unless wearing long dress.

3. Do not smoke or drink alcohol.

4. Do not commit adultery.

5. Do not use pork in any form.

6. Do not cook in aluminum utensils.

7. Do not wear heels over $1\frac{1}{2}$ inches.

8. Do not dance with anyone except one's husband.

Young boys are expected to be members of the Fruit of Islam, which is divided into age groups: for children and adolescents from 1 to 16 years old, from 16 to 35 years old, and men over 35. Each Temple has a unit of the Fruit of Islam. A captain leads it and has a staff composed of several lieutenants, drill masters, and secretaries. Members are also trained in self-defense techniques. The purpose of the Fruit of Islam is three-fold:

1. To protect organizational officials and property;

2. To reinforce the doctrine and objective of the organization;

3. To prepare for the race war known as Armageddon.

There is a nominal tuition charge at the University of Islam. The organization also provides adult education classes for its members.

The period from 1935 to 1946 represented difficult times in the development of the Nation of Islam. When the United States entered World War II, Elijah Muhammad was arrested and found guilty for refusing to comply with the Selective Service Act. Elijah Muhammad, his son Emmanuel, and several other Muslims were charged " ... with evading the draft and influencing others to do so, and also with maintaining relations with the Japanese government. The later indictment more or less petered out."[28]

Elijah Muhammad was sentenced to the federal penitentiary in Milan, Michigan, and served four years, from 1942 to 1946. Elijah and Emmanuel established a Temple in the penitentiary, where they held services on Wednesday and Friday evenings and Sunday afternoons.   They made many converts in prison.   Many Muslims would leave one prison and convert others; once released, they would join the Temple in their communities.

While Elijah and Emmanuel were in prison, Clara Muhammad, Elijah's wife, was instrumental in keeping the movement together.   Clara Muhammad was the supreme secretary of the movement during Elijah Muhammad's incarceration. The " ... orders came from him [Elijah Muhammad] to her to the ministers and captains.   She was executing his decision for him while he was in prison."29

Elijah Muhammad's imprisonment appeared a martyrdom to his followers and it enhanced his position upon his release from the federal penetentiary.   He returned to Chicago as the undisputed leader of the Nation of Islam.

When Elijah Muhammad was paroled from prison, there was one temple each in Detroit, Chicago, Milwaukee, and Washington, D.C.   In the 1950's the Nation of Islam began to establish temples throughout the country.   A primary reason for expansion of the organization was the recruitment of a former inmate named Malcolm Little.   In 1948 Malcolm Little was serving a ten-year prison term for grand larceny in the Norfolk Prison Colony in Massachusetts.   During this time his older brother, Philbert, joined the Nation of Islam and began to correspond with him on the "natural religion for the black man."   Malcolm began to correspond with Elijah Muhammad and read Muslim literature.   Malcolm, known as Satan by fellow inmates because of his anti-religious beliefs, began to pray to Allah.   One night Malcolm had a vision " ... of a man with a light-brown skin, an Asiatic countenance and oily-black hair sitting beside his prison bed."30   Malcolm believed the man in his vision was W.D. Fard.

During the spring of 1952 Malcolm Little was paroled from prison and went to Detroit Temple #1.   He joined the Nation of Islam and received his X.   Malcolm " ... came right out of prison and became a minister; he didn't take on the thinking and behavior of the old conservative ministerial body."31   Minister Malcolm, " ... became a familiar figure on Harlem street corners, holding large audiences spellbound."32

In 1959 Malcolm X created the organization's newspaper, Muhammad Speaks, which was an extension of Elijah Muhammad's column in the Pittsburgh Courier, the Los Angeles Herald Dispatch, the Chicago Defender, and the Chicago News Crusader.   It had a circulation of over 500,000.   During the same year Malcolm X was appointed National Spokesman by Elijah Muhammad.   Elijah Muhammad recognized the appeal of the tall, handsome, and articulate Malcolm X and often told his older ministers, "You're teaching the same thing we taught in the thirties.   Malcolm X is in modern times; he knows how to help me."[33]   Malcolm X emerged as the major voice of the Nation of Islam.   His appointment as National Spokesman made Malcolm X the leading figure in the organization.   Elijah Muhammad " ... welcomed this new blood. He gave Malcolm free reign to preach his doctrine."[34]   Slowly Malcolm X began to alter the doctrine and influence membership on the virtues of Orthodox Islam.   The transformation from black Muslims to Muslims began in the early 1960's with the emerging leadership of Malcolm X.

Chapter V will describe the contribution of Malcolm X to the development of the Nation of Islam.

PROGRAM AND POSITION

What Muslims Want:

1) We want freedom.   We want a full, complete freedom.

2) We want justice, equal justice under the law.   We want justice applied equally regardless of creed, class or color.

3) We want equality of opportunity.

4) We want our people in America whose parents or grandparents were descendants from slaves to be allowed to establish a separate state or territory of their own.

5) We want freedom of all believers of Islam now held in federal prison.

6) We want an immediate end to the police brutality and mob attacks against the so-called Negroes throughout the United States.

7) As long as we are not allowed to establish a state or territory of our own, we demand not only equal justice under the laws of the United States, but equal employment opportunities now!

8) We want the government of the United States to exempt our people from all taxation as long as we are deprived of equal justice under the laws of the land.

9) We want equal education--but separate schools, up to sixteen for boys and eighteen for girls on the condition that the girls be sent to women's colleges and universities. We want all black children educated, taught and trained by their own teachers.

What Muslims Believe:

1) We believe in the one God whose proper name is Allah.

2) We believe in the Holy Koran and in the scriptures of all the prophets of God.

3) We believe in the truth of the Bible, but we believe that it has been tampered with and must be reinterpreted so that mankind will not be snared by the falsehoods that have been added to it.

4) We believe in Allah's prophets and the scriptures they brought to the people.

5) We believe in the resurrection of the dead--not in physical resurrection--but in mental resurrection. We believe that the so-called Negroes are most in need of mental resurrection. Therefore, they will be resurrected first. Furthermore, we believe we are the people of God's choice.

6) We believe in the judgment, we believe this first judgment will take place as God revealed, in America.

7) We believe this is the time in history for the separation of the so-called Negroes and the so-called white Americans.

8) We believe in justice for all, whether in God or not; we believe as others, that we are due equal justice as human beings. We believe in equality--as a nation--of equals. We do not believe that we are equal with our slave masters in the status of "freed slaves." We recognize and respect American citizens as independent people and we respect their laws which govern this nation.

9) We believe that the offer of integration is hypocritical and is made by those who are trying to deceive the black people into believing that their 400-year-old open enemies of freedom, justice, and equality are, all of a sudden, their "friends."

10) We believe that intermarriage or race-mixing should be prohibited.

11) We believe that we who declared ourselves to be righteous Muslims should not participate in wars which take the lives of humans.

12) We believe our women should be respected and protected as the women of other nationalities are respected and protected.

13) We believe that Allah (God) appeared in the person of Master W. Fard Muhammad, July 1930; the long awaited "Messiah" of the Christians and the "Mahdi" of the Muslims.

NOTES

1. Interview, Imam Wallace D. Muhammad, Chicago, Illinois, July 25, 1979.

2. Arna Bontemps and Jack Conroy, They Seek a City (New York: Doubleday, 1945), p. 217.

3. Ibid.

4. Interview, Charles 4X Jackson, member of the Nation of Islam, Los Angeles, California, April 4, 1970.

5. Interview, Imam Wallace D. Muhammad.

6. Interview, James 2X Jones, member of the Nation of Islam, Richmond, Virginia, July 5, 1976.

7. Interview, Imam Wallace D. Muhammad.

8. Ibid.

9. Elijah Muhammad, Message to the Blackman in America (Chicago: Muhammad's Mosque #2, 1965), pp. 178-179.

10. Muhammad Speaks, Special Issue, April 1972.

11. Interview, Imam Wallace D. Muhammad.

12. Eric C. Lincoln, The Black Muslims in America (Canada: Saunders of Toronto, 1961), p. 15.

13. Theodore Draper, The Rediscovery of Black Nationalism (New York: Viking Press, 1969), p. 79.

14. Muhammad, Message, p. 120.

15. Lincoln, Black Muslims, p. 13.

16. Muhammad, Message, p. 183.

17. Interview, Imam Wallace D. Muhammad.

18. Ibid.

19. Ibid.

20. Bontemps and Conroy, They Seek, p. 228.

21. Draper, Rediscovery, p. 84.

22. Interview, Charles 4X Jackson.

23. Muhammad, Message, p. XIV.

24. Ibid.

25. E. U. Essien-Udom, Black Nationalism: A Search for an Identity in America (Chicago: University of Chicago Press, 1962), p. 286.

26.   Interview, Sharon Shabazz, Nation of Islam, New York City, December 16, 1975.

27.   Muhammad, Message, p. 174.

28.   Bontemps and Conroy, They Seek, p. 224.

29.   Interview, Imam Wallace D. Muhammad.

30.   Draper, Rediscovery, p. 84.

31.   Interview, Imam Wallace D. Muhammad.

32.   Bontemps and Conroy, They Seek, p. 232.

33.   Interview, Imam Wallace D. Muhammad.

34.   Ibid.

Chapter V

MINISTER MALCOLM X SHABAZZ

> "Minister Malcolm's contribution to the changes
> that took place in the Nation of Islam goes fur-
> ther back than my own. When I was a young
> man, maybe the early twenties, Malcolm X was
> an influence in my life."
>
> --Imam Wallace D.
> Muhammad, Chief
> Minister, WCIW

Malcolm X Shabazz was a leading spokesman in the struggle
for human rights. His influence and charisma transcended
the Nation of Islam and the domicile of the United States.

By the time Minister Malcolm X met his death via an
assassin's bullet, he had become an international leader.
Imam Wallace D. Muhammad's quote above attests to Malcolm's significance in the alteration of the Nation of Islam's
ideology. Malcolm X Shabazz was the chief spokesman and
traveling representative of Elijah Muhammad for 12 years.
Malcolm's dynamic personality and articulate speaking was
instrumental in recruiting, organizing temples, and providing
exposure domestically and internationally for the Nation of
Islam. Most of Malcolm's career was associated with developing and propagating the ideology of the Nation of Islam.

Malcolm brought youth, individuality, and often conflict
during the caucuses of Elijah Muhammad's ministerial body.
Initially, Elijah Muhammad welcomed and encouraged Malcolm.
Eventually Malcolm's intellectual growth and the changing cur-

rent of the African-American and Third World struggle drove
a wedge between Malcolm and Elijah Muhammad.

Malcolm adopted three names during his life; each represented an evolutionary stage in his ideological development
and life-style. "Pulled from the mud" by a religious conversion in prison, Malcolm Little, or "Detroit Red," as he was
known, was a pimp, racketeer, and dope pusher. After his
acceptance of the Nation of Islam's doctrine, Malcolm X became a black nationalist devoted to the separatist teachings
of Elijah Muhammad. When he defected from the "Black
Muslims" and accepted Orthodox Islam, Malcolm then adopted
the name El Hajj Malik El-Shabazz.

Malcolm described his life as one of changes. Where
Malcolm would have gone ideologically, had he not been assassinated, can only be guessed. He was in the process of
developing his new perspective before his death. Where he
came from and what he did in his lifetime is a remarkable
biography.

Malcolm Little was born May 19, 1925, in Omaha,
Nebraska. His father, the Reverend Earl Little, was tall
(six feet four inches) and "very very dark." Malcolm's mother, Louise, was born in Grenada, which was then a British
colony in the Caribbean.

The Little family consisted of eight children; Earl supported them as a free-lance Baptist minister. He also was
an organizer for Marcus Garvey's Universal Negro improvement Association. Young Malcolm often accompanied his father to UNIA meetings and was impressed as the Garveyites
exclaimed, "Africa for Africans and Ethiopia Awake."

Reverend Little raised the ire of the local white community because of his attempts to organize black people in
Omaha. Their home was burned to the ground one evening by
the Ku Klux Klan while he was away.

Shortly after the birth of Malcolm the Littles moved to
Milwaukee and eventually to Lansing, Michigan. When Malcolm was six years old his father was murdered. "He was
attacked and then laid across some tracks for a street car to
run over him."[1] Malcolm believed that he, too, would die a
violent death as so many men in his family had.

Louise Little raised her eight children during the Depression. Eventually, the strain of poverty and the dehuman-

izing welfare system rendered Mrs. Little helpless. She suffered, " ... a complete breakdown and the court orders were
finally signed. They took her to the state mental hospital at
Kalamazoo. "[2] Mrs. Little remained in the hospital for twenty-
six years. The children were supported in state institutions,
boarding homes, or lived with relatives.

During his elementary school years, Malcolm Little
was an exceptional student. He was the only black person in
his class at Mason Junior High School and was elected class
president in the seventh grade. Malcolm participated in bas-
ketball and, urged on by the success of his brother Philbert,
boxed as a bantamweight. Malcolm's height and rawboned
frame enabled him to deceive the officials into believing he
was 16 years old--even though he was just 13 at that time.
His boxing career ended when he was knocked out twice by
the "same white boy."

During a Careers Day at Mason Junior High, Malcolm
was reprimanded by his counselor for aspiring to become a
lawyer. The school counselor suggested carpentry as a realistic occupation for a "nigger."

From that moment on, Malcolm became alienated from
school, Lansing, and white America. He began corresponding
with his older sister Ella in Boston, requesting to live with
her. Ella gained official custody of Malcolm, transferring
him from Michigan to Massachusetts.

The move from Lansing to Boston was the beginning of
Malcolm's street education which catapulted him into a life of
crime. Between the ages of 15 and 21, Malcolm spent his
life in the ghettos of Boston and Harlem engaged in part-time
"legal" employment--drugs, gambling, and hustling.

Ella lived in the Sugar Hill section of Roxbury, which
was largely black middle-class, but the life-style of the urban
poor and working class attracted young Malcolm like a mag-
net.

Malcolm's first job was shining shoes in the Roseland
State Ballroom where he unscuffed the toes of great musicians
like Duke Ellington, Count Basie, Lionel Hampton, and Lester
Young. While employed at Roseland, Malcolm began to smoke
marijuana, play numbers, wear zoot suits, "conk" his hair
red, and dance a frantic Lindy Hop. Malcolm left Roseland
and was employed by the railroad as the fourth cook on the

Yankee Clipper, which traveled between Boston and New York
City. Malcolm's first visit to Harlem narcotized him. In
Small's Paradise Bar Malcolm said, he was " ... awed within
the first five minutes in Small's; I had left Boston and Roxbury forever."3

In 1942, at the age of 17, he quit his railroad job and
became a waiter in Small's. Malcolm Little was on his way
to becoming " ... one of the most depraved, parasitical hust-
lers among New York's eight million people."4   Malcolm was
eventually fired and barred from Small's for procuring a pros-
titute for a serviceman while in the resturant.

When Malcolm was dismissed from Small's, he turned
to crime for full-time employment and acquired the name "Detroit Red." Initially he sold reefers (marijuana cigarettes),
but within six months Malcolm began to engage in armed rob-
bery. Armed with a .32, .38 or .45 pistol and snorting co-
caine for courage, "Detroit Red" prowled the streets looking
for victims.

Malcolm was almost 21 before he was arrested and
sentenced to up to ten years on a burglary charge. In February of 1946 Malcolm Little was sent to Charlestown State
Prison and in 1948 he was transferred to the Norfolk Prison
Colony. He served a total of six years in prison.

Malcolm Little underwent a religious conversion in prison, with encouraging words from his family to "face east
and pray to Allah." Malcolm began to investigate the Nation
of Islam and correspond with Elijah Muhammad. Malcolm
spent most of his time studying, researching, and developing
his penmanship. He took correspondence courses in English
and Latin and developed his vocabulary by memorizing a dic-
tionary. Malcolm developed his political consciousness by
reading volumes of African and African-American history and
Oriental philosophy. He eventually led prison debates and
discussion groups which enhanced his public speaking.

Malcolm Little was released on parole at the age of 27
after six years in prison. When he was released in August
of 1952, he was a "Black Muslim," although he had not acquired his X. By writing Elijah Muhammad weekly and being
counseled by his brothers, Wilfred and Philbert, "Detroit Red"
became a devoted follower of Elijah Muhammad. He spent the
next 12 years totally devoted to the Nation of Islam and mesmerized by Elijah Muhammad.

Throughout his career as a Muslim, Malcolm was a diligent recruiter, tireless worker (he routinely worked 18-hour days), and devout Muslim. His Pan-African ideology and Orthodox Islamic beliefs developed later in his career as he studied and traveled domestically and abroad.

Malcolm moved to Detroit after his parole to live with his brother Wilfred. There he received his X in Temple #1, the original temple organized by Wali Fard Muhammad. The Detroit Temple was located in a storefront at 1470 Frederick Street. Most of Muhammad's Temples were located in the urban black community. During the early years of the Nation of Islam, the organization owned very little property, so most of the Temples were rented halls, frequently on the second floor of a commercial establishment. The Chicago Headquarters and the Washington, D.C. Temples are notable exceptions since they were built and owned by the Nation of Islam.

It was the practice each month for the Detroit Temple to motorcade caravan-style to Chicago to hear sermons by Elijah Muhammad. The Sunday before Labor Day in 1952, a two-car caravan transported Malcolm X and several ministers to Chicago.

During this period Malcolm was employed by the Garwood Furniture Company and later as an assemblyman with the Ford Motor Company. Every evening after work Malcolm walked the ghetto looking for new recruits in bars, pool rooms, and on street corners.

Malcolm's aggressive tactics tripled the membership and in a few months he lead a caravan of twenty-five automobiles to Chicago to hear Elijah Muhammad speak. Needless to say, Elijah Muhammad was very pleased by the increased membership generated by the converted ex-convict, Malcolm X. During the summer of 1953, Malcolm X was appointed Assistant Minister of Temple #1 and became a full-time minister for the Nation of Islam.

In larger Temples, ministers devote all their time to organization activities. The minister receives support from donations made by Temple members and his home, car, and family necessities are supplied by the Temple membership. Ministers in smaller Temples work a full-time job to support themselves.

Malcolm X began to serve as Elijah Muhammad's Prime

Minister throughout the United States, going from city to city
preaching, recruiting, and establishing new Temples. In the
1950's a period of expansion began for the Nation of Islam.
Malcolm X helped to establish most of the one hundred Temples in the United States. He was " ... crisscrossing North
America, sometimes as often as four times a week."[5] From
Detroit, Malcolm X was sent to Boston to organize Temple
#11. In March 1954 Malcolm moved from Boston to Philadel-
phia and in three months Temple #12 was opened in the City
of Brotherly Love. From Philadelphia, Malcolm X moved to
New York City and became minister of Temple #7.

Malcolm X returned to New York, where a few short
years before his colleagues had been West Indian Archie, Sam-
my the Pimp, and Cadillac Drake. Clean-shaven and walking
tall in suit and tie, his former friends in crime exclaimed in
disbelief, "Red, my man! This can't be you!"

From the storefront of Temple #7 Malcolm roamed the
boroughs of New York recruiting on street corners, in Christian churches, and in other nationalist groups. On weekdays
he traveled by bus and train to preach in other parts of the
country. Many times he preached in private homes until the
membership became large enough to rent a Temple.

Malcolm's impatience with older, more conservative
ministers and the pace of the development of the organization
provoked Elijah Muhammad to chastise him often.

Malcolm wanted to recruit more followers, build more
Temples, and hire better ministers. Malcolm believed he increased the membership from 400 to 40,000 in the few years
after he joined. Elijah Muhammad needed Malcolm's charisma
and organizational skills, but he also had to temper his en-
thusiasm.

The only thing that kept Malcolm under control during
his early years was his complete devotion and trust in Elijah
Muhammad and Malcolm's own ideological development. Though
chastising Malcolm as he did, Elijah Muhammad continued to
support Malcolm's evangelistic style.

In 1955 Malcolm organized Temple #15 in Atlanta,
Georgia. To reward and assist the young minister, the Nation of Islam supplied him with a new 1956 Chevrolet. Malcolm X put 30,000 miles on the automobile in five months.
In 1957 Elijah Muhammad sent Malcolm X west where he organized the Los Angeles Temple.

Prior to Malcolm's tenure, the Nation of Islam was successful in recruiting poor and working class black people, but few educated and skilled individuals joined their ranks. By 1957 the Nation of Islam began to attract the educated, academics, people with vocational skills, civil servants, nurses, and clerical and sales persons. A more remarkable metamorphosis appeared among the ministers of the Nation of Islam. Elijah Muhammad was often perturbed over his inability to attract younger, educated people in general and younger, educated ministers in particular.

Imam Wallace D. Muhammad explained how Malcolm persuaded the youth to follow Elijah Muhammad: "Malcolm's new thinking, courage and youth attracted most of the young people into following the Honorable Elijah Muhammad and I was one of them."[6]

In examining the education and background of the nine most active ministers, there is a distinct difference between the type of ministers active prior to Malcolm and the type that joined the organization after Malcolm.

Four of the nine ministers were members of the Nation of Islam prior to 1953, James 3X Anderson, Chicago; James 3X McGregor, Newark; Isaiah Karriem Edwards, Baltimore; and Wilfred X Little (Malcolm's brother), Detroit.

Anderson, McGregor, and Edwards became Muslims in the early 1940's and each served a prison term for refusing to register for the military draft. Each had been a Muslim for years before attaining the status of minister. The fourth minister was Malcolm's brother Wilfred who, though a member of the Nation of Islam prior to 1953, had not yet risen to a leadership position. The remaining five of the nine leading ministers joined the Nation of Islam after Malcolm became a leading official. They were Lonnie 3X Cross, Washington, D.C.; Bernard X Cushmere, San Francisco; John Shabazz, Los Angeles; Jeremiah X Pugh, Philadelphia; and Louis X Walcott, who eventually succeeded Malcolm X as National Spokesman, Boston. All of these ministers had at least a high school or college education, one being a Ph.D. and a former college professor. Louis X Walcott was a former calypso singer, poet, and playwright. Their average age was 33. Seven of the nine ministers owed their conversion to Malcolm and were assisted by him in gaining their leadership status.

The influential ministerial body was significant, but

still subordinate to Elijah Muhammad and the Nation of Islam's hierarchy stationed in Chicago. The organization's elite leaders consisted of most of the members of Elijah Muhammad's immediate family: Hassan Sharrieff, Mr. Elijah Muhammad's grandson, was in charge of public relations; Herbert Muhammad--publisher of Muhammad Speaks; Elijah Muhammad, Jr.--Assistant Supreme Captain of the Fruit of Islam; Raymond Sharriff, Elijah's son-in-law (married Elijah's daughter Ethel)--Supreme Captain of the Fruit of Islam; and Wallace Muhammad--Minister-at-Large. Elijah Muhammad's daughter Lottie Fagan and sons Emmanuel and Nathaniel were also devoted to their father and his message. The only non-family member among national leaders was John Ali, who was the National Secretary.

Through Malcolm's training and recruitment of top ministers, he was indirectly shaping the destiny of the organization. The family hierarchy, however, was devoted to Elijah Muhammad.

During this period, Elijah Muhammad's very ambitious three-year economic plan began to bear fruit. Numerous small-business service enterprises began to emerge under the aegis of the Nation of Islam. Bakeries, restaurants, dress shops, barbershops, grocery stores and cleaning establishments. The businesses derived most of their income from members of the organization and from residents of the black community patronizing the Muslim enterprises.

On January 14, 1958, Malcolm X married Sister Betty X, a tall brown-skinned beauty and former student at Tuskegee Institute in Alabama. The family grew to include four daughters, Attilah (1958), Qubilah (1960), Ilyasah (1962), and Amilah (1964).

In 1959, the media played an important role in providing the Nation of Islam and Malcolm X with national and international recognition. Newsman Mike Wallace, with the help of a black writer, Louis Lomay, persuaded the Nation of Islam to participate in a television documentary entitled, "The Hate That Hate Produced," which brought the organization into homes of millions of television viewers. Also, Malcolm began to speak before a wider audience by appearing on college campuses, and radio and television talk shows. The organization received coverage in Life, Look, Newsweek, Time and Reader's Digest.

Malcolm was still a devoted and obedient follower of Elijah Muhammad, echoing his doctrine wherever he spoke. Beginning each response with "The Honorable Elijah Muhammad teaches us," he would espouse the virtues of separation for the black man in America as the only solution.

Malcolm X believed that the American economic and political system was unequal and unjust and that to integrate into such a system would do nothing for the masses of poor and working class blacks. Only through separation (not segregation, which results in white control of the black community) would true equality be created because " ... separation is that which is done voluntarily by two equals for the good of both."[7]

Malcolm also felt that Christianity assisted in the subordination of blacks and still insisted "Christianity is the white man's religion." The Bible in the " ... white man's hands and his interpretations of it, have been the greatest single ideological weapon for enslaving millions of non-white human beings."[8]

On matters of race, Malcolm still parroted the doctrine initiated by Wali Fard and carried on by Elijah Muhammad. Malcolm still believed that "Our enemy is the white man!" and he equated the "enemy" with the devil. "Oh yes, that devil is our enemy," he would preach.

As late as 1959 he broadened the concept from purely race and color classification to actions and behavior. Malcolm explained, "We are not speaking of any individual white man. We are speaking of the collective white man's historical record. The white man's collective cruelties, evils and deeds, that have seen him act like a devil toward the non-white man."[9]

Because Elijah Muhammad was confined to Phoenix, Arizona, in 1959 for his bronchial condition, he was unable to regulate the decision-making and administrative duties of the Nation of Islam. He carried on the work through his family members and loyal ministers and eventually appointed Malcolm X National Spokesman. Elijah gave Malcolm the opportunity to make his own decisions in governing the affairs of the Nation of Islam. Malcolm stated, "He said that my guideline should be whatever I felt was wise--whatever was in the general good interests of our Nation of Islam."[10]

Entering the 1960's the stage was set for Malcolm to emerge from the shadow of Elijah Muhammad and become an international leader. There were several reasons for Malcolm's prominence during that decade. Malcolm's appointment as National Spokesman provided a platform for him as the charismatic leader. The increased administrative and decision-making duties gave Malcolm more power to utilize the numerous institutions within the Nation of Islam. Media coverage of the organization's activities provided massive exposure and Malcolm was the natural focal point.

The rise of black nationalism in the 1960's in the United States came during the escalation of the Vietnam War and liberation struggles in Colonial Africa. The nationalist leaders perceived the African-American struggle in world solidarity as a struggle against colonialism, racism, and capitalist expansionism. The Nation of Islam was the oldest and most powerful black nationalist organization in the United States. Malcolm X became the "Prince of the Black Revolution."

With the mood of nationalism sweeping black America, Malcolm felt the Nation of Islam should be active in leading a frontline struggle. Malcolm was convinced " ... that the Nation of Islam could be even a greater force in the American Black man's overall struggle if we engaged in more action. "[11]. Elijah Muhammad advocated that Muslims should not become involved in the "white man's politics" and insisted that members invest their time on self-improvement. Malcolm perceived the self-improvement position as making the Nation of Islam a separate, closed community within the black community. Malcolm even considered voting as a means of achieving power. He said, "The polls are one place where every black man could fight the black man's cause with dignity and power. "[12]

In April 1960 Elijah Muhammad's son Wallace was sentenced to prison for three years for failure to report for hospital work as a conscientious objector. For the next three years, Elijah Muhammad spent over $20,000 in legal fees appealing the decision. On November 4, 1961, Wallace entered prison. Even before he entered prison Wallace had doubts about his father's version of Islam. Wallace also questioned his father's interpretation of Wali Fard as Allah. Wallace had seen many of Fard's writings in which he referred to himself as the messenger of Allah.

The same year that Wallace went to prison, Malcolm began to encounter jealousy and hostility within the hierarchy of the Nation of Islam. Most of the problems emanated from the National Headquarters in Chicago. Rumors were spread that "Malcolm is trying to take over the Nation." He was accused of taking credit for Elijah Muhammad's teachings and building a financial empire. The media, black leaders and even several Muslims were giving Malcolm credit for the progress of the Nation of Islam.

In response to the rumors and accusations, Malcolm began refusing interviews and public addresses. He often urged the media to "Please use Mr. Muhammad's picture instead of mine." By 1962, Malcolm noticed he appeared less and less in the organization's newspaper, Muhammad Speaks. Herbert Muhammad, the publisher of the paper, instructed editors to "print as little as possible about Malcolm." Malcolm began to resent these efforts after the hard work he had performed for the organization. Eventually, he received no coverage at all in Muhammad Speaks. In addition, the Chicago headquarters began to discourage him from holding rallies and public speaking engagements.

In January 10, 1963, Wallace D. Muhammad was paroled from Sandstone Correctional Institution. While in prison, Wallace meditated, discussed and wrote about Islam, and made comparisons with his father's version of the religion. Wallace consulted several relatives and organization members (including Malcolm X) to clarify his doubts about his father's teachings. Wallace regularly attended Nation of Islam functions and taught classes at the University of Islam. Wallace stirred up much controversy concerning his father's activities both nationally and in Chicago.

During the same year, Elijah Muhammad became a subject of rumors concerning his morality. A UPI press release stated that testimony by two of Elijah Muhammad's former secretaries, Miss Rosary and Miss Williams, indicated they had sexual relationships with Mr. Muhammad since 1957. Each woman alleged that Elijah Muhammad had fathered their children. Malcolm X had utmost faith in Elijah Muhammad and perceived him as the symbol or moral and spiritual reform for African Americans. These rumors forced Malcolm to discuss morality less during public speaking engagements and concentrate on social doctrine, current events, and politics.

To satisfy his own curiosity and possibly stop the ru-

mors, Malcolm X launched his own investigation. He interviewed the membership, family members, and three former
secretaries; they all confirmed the rumors.

For advice, Malcolm X confided in Wallace D. Muhammad. Wallace and Malcolm reviewed the Koran and the Bible
for documentation and biblical justification for Elijah Muhammad's actions. With Wallace's help Malcolm found Koran and
Bible passages that might be taught to the membership as the
fulfillment of prophecy. Malcolm visited Elijah Muhammad
in Chicago and asked him about the accusations by the two
secretaries. Elijah Muhammad was pleased with Malcolm's
koranic and biblical research. He replied,

> I'm David, when you read about how David took
> another man's wife, I'm that David. You read
> about Noah, who got drunk--that's me. You read
> about Lot, who went and laid up with his own daugh-
> ter. I have fulfilled all those things."[13]

Malcolm's concern was interpreted as spreading dissension and fanning flames of discontent. Resentment and
hostility toward Malcolm rapidly increased among numerous
members of the "Royal Family." When it appeared Malcolm
was becoming more powerful and influential than Elijah Muhammad, the leadership in Chicago began to sever Malcolm's
powers within the organization. Malcolm was being forced
out of the leadership circle and eventually the organization.
Malcolm was aggressive, eager, and articulate and was often
moving faster than Elijah Muhammad wished, as well as moving in political directions that Elijah Muhammad did not ap-
prove. Malcolm was gaining more and more prominence
within the organization. Domestically and abroad, he became
better known than any black leader in the United States, including Elijah Muhammad.

Malcolm X's ideological growth began to ripen by 1963.
He started to question more and more the Nation of Islam's
doctrine, political activities (or lack of them), and religious
beliefs. Malcolm began to detour from Elijah Muhammad's
doctrine and addressed social and economic issues oppressing
black people domestically and internationally. He began to
speak out against the United States government for its involvement in the Vietnam War and the lack of commitment toward
solving domestic problems.

On November 22, 1963, President John F. Kennedy was

assassinated. Afterwards, Elijah Muhammad issued a directive to all Muslim ministers to refrain from commenting on his death. In a speaking engagement in New York's Manhattan Center during a question and answer period, Malcolm X was asked his opinion of the assassination. He replied, "I saw it, as a case of chickens coming home to roost. I said it was the same thing as had happened with Medgar Evers, with Patrice Lumumba, with Madam Nhu's husband."[14]

Malcolm X was silenced for ninety days by Elijah Muhammad for making these remarks. For a month after the silencing many conferences were held between Malcolm, Elijah Muhammad, and national leaders. The differences between Malcolm and the Nation of Islam became more pronounced. Elijah Muhammad removed Malcolm as a minister of Temple #7 in New York in January 1964. The same month, Muhammad excommunicated his son Wallace for working closely with Malcolm. Wallace explained the excommunication, "I was charged with trying to influence Malcolm's theological thinking and with giving him personal private knowledge of the Honorable Elijah Muhammad's living."[15] Wallace protested the excommunication to no avail. He wanted to face his accusers, but Muhammad declared, "Malcolm X is not facing his accusers either."

The following month, a young Louisville heavyweight was training in Miami, Florida, to fight Sonny Liston for the Heavyweight Championship of the World. The young challenger, Cassius Clay, invited Malcolm X and his family to his training camp to honor Malcolm and Betty on their sixth wedding anniversary. Malcolm had known Cassius as early as 1962 when Cassius and his brother Rudolph came to Detroit to hear Elijah Muhammad speak; they consequently became close friends.

Young Clay won a gold medal in the 1960 Rome Olympics. When he returned home to Kentucky, he and his friend, Ronnie King, were refused service in a restaurant because they were black. After leaving the restaurant, Clay and King were attacked by a white motorcycle gang which Clay and King fought off. Discouraged and angry, Clay heaved his gold medal into the Ohio River as a silent protest. Clay became interested in the Nation of Islam shortly afterward. In 1962, Cassius and Rudolph attended several Nation of Islam functions throughout the country. Cassius even spoke before a Nation of Islam rally in January 1964 while training for the Sonny Liston fight.

Clay's "I-am-the-greatest" antics brought him considerable news coverage. Prior to the fight with Sonny Liston on February 25, 1964, no one gave Cassius Clay a chance to survive with his life, much less win the fight. Prior to the fight, in Clay's dressing room, Malcolm X gave young Clay a religious pep talk. Malcolm yelled, "This fight is truth; it's the Cross and the Crescent fighting."[16] Malcolm terminated his pep talk with a question to Clay. He peered into his sweat-soaked face and asked, "Do you think Allah has brought about all this, intending for you to leave the ring anything but a champion?"[17] Malcolm and the young contender faced east and prayed to Allah.

Malcolm X left Cassius Clay's dressing room and took a seat among 8,000 fans at Miami's Convention Hall. The "Louisville Lip" shocked the sports world and won by a technical knockout in the seventh round. The bleeding and exhausted Sonny Liston was unable to leave his stool to answer the bell for the seventh round. After the fight, Clay announced, "I believe in the religion of Islam which means I believe there is no God but Allah and Muhammad is his apostle."[18]

Soon after the fight, newspapers carried pictures with Malcolm X introducing Cassius Clay to numerous African diplomats in the United Nations. Malcolm and Clay rode through Harlem and other parts of the country with Malcolm as the champion's friend and religious advisor. On March 6, 1964, Elijah Muhammad bestowed on Clay the name Muhammad Ali. Malcolm predicted that Muhammad Ali would, " ... develop into a major world figure."

By 1964, Malcolm X and the Nation of Islam's marriage of 12 years was breaking up. Malcolm felt he would remain suspended and eventually be "isolated," excluded from all Muslim functions. Malcolm also began receiving rumors of his assassination and suspected a zealous follower of Elijah Muhammad might kill him as his religious duty.

On March 8, 1964, Malcolm accounced he was leaving the Nation of Islam to establish his own organization based upon Orthodox Islamic principles called the Muslim Mosque Inc. with an associate political body, the Organization of Afro-American Unity. Malcolm's organization consisted of approximately 50 former Nation of Islam members. The headquarters for his organization was the Hotel Theresa on 125th Street and Seventh Avenue in Harlem. The organization of Afro-American

unity was a " ... non-religious and non-sectarian group organized to unite Afro-Americans for a constructive program
toward attainment of human rights. "[19]   The OAAU was an
all-black organization whose ultimate objective was to " ...
help create a society in which there could be an honest white-
black brotherhood. "[20]   Malcolm was willing to work with white
people and requested their financial support.   He urged whites
to confront racism in their own communities to create a brotherhood of all races.   However, Malcolm did not permit whites
to join the OAAU.   He was convinced there could be no black
and white coalitions before black solidarity was achieved.   Ultimately, black and white organizations would have solidarity,
but only after African Americans had been organized.   Malcolm traveled extensively to Africa and his ideological growth
accelerated.

In April 1964, Malcolm X made the pilgrimage, known
as the Hajj, to the Holy City of Mecca.   Muslims are obligated to take at least one pilgrimage in their lifetime, if financially able.   During his pilgrimage, Malcolm began to alter his perspective on the Nation of Islam's doctrine and Islam practiced by Muslims throughout the world.   Malcolm was
embarrassed because, as a Muslim minister, he did not know
the prayer ritual, nor did he practice the "Pillars of Islam"
and other Islamic principles.   He was impressed with the spirit of brotherhood, lack of color-consciousness and non-racist
attitudes among Muslims.   He met with Islamic scholars and
read volumes of literature on the religion.

The following month, Malcolm X went on an 18-week
trip through Africa and had private audiences with several
African Heads of State.   In Egypt Malcolm was the guest of
King Faisal and also talked to Gamal Abdel Nasser of Egypt,
President Julius K. Nyere of Tanzania, President Nnamai
Asikiwe of Nigeria, Dr. Kwame Nkrumah of Ghana, President
Jomo Kenyatta of Kenya, and Prime Minister Dr. Milton Obote
of Uganda.   Malcolm's travels convinced him that Islam as
taught by Elijah Muhammad was out of sync with 800 million
Muslims worldwide.   His discussions with Wallace D. Muham-
mad made Malcolm suspect the Nation of Islam was an unorthodox brand of Islam.   The Hajj reinforced his suspicions and
resulted in his conversion to Orthodox Islam.

When Malcolm X returned to the United States in June
1964, he found there was still dissension within the ranks of
the Royal Family of Muhammad.   On June 21, 1964, Elijah
Muhammad's grandson Hassan Sharrieff was expelled from the

organization and denounced as a hypocrite for deviating from
Elijah Muhammad's teachings. On January 1, 1965, another
of Elijah Muhammad's sons was expelled; Akbar Muhammad's
expulsion followed after he refused to denounce Wallace and
Malcolm as hypocrites. Instead of denouncing Malcolm and
Wallace he praised them. Akbar was a student of Islamic
Law at Al Azhar University in Cairo, Egypt. He referred
to his father's brand of Islam as "homemade" and not an ac-
curate reflection of the religion. Eventually Akbar and his
family returned to Egypt.

The conflict within the Nation of Islam convinced Malcolm X he was correct in his analysis of the organization and
his political and ideological development. Malcolm changed
his name to El Hajj Malik El-Shabazz after he accepted Orthodox Islam. Malcolm felt true Islam unites people rather than
separating them as Elijah Muhammad's teaching advocated.

Betty Shabazz, Malcolm X's wife, described her husband's change, "He went to Mecca as a Black Muslim and
there he became only a Muslim. He felt all men were human
beings; we must judge a man on his deeds."[21] Malcolm Shabazz felt the Muslim world's religious community and the societies built upon Islamic principles had eliminated racism.
He began to separate whiteness as a color from attitudes and
actions. Malcolm truly believed color and race were irrele-
vant in the Muslim world but, " ... if one encountered any
difference based on attitudes toward color, this directly re-
flected the degree of Western influence."[22]

Malcolm Shabazz' changed attitude toward white people
was based upon his international travels and observing other
social systems and economic means of production. By virtue
of his observations he believed that capitalism and racism are
related by reinforcing racial inequality for private gain. It
was not white people per se who were inherently evil, but the
United States' political, economic, and social system which
was demonic. Malcolm said, " ... the American political,
economic and social atmosphere ... automatically nourishes
a racist psychology in the white man."[23]

Malcolm Shabazz' travels throughout Africa convinced
him to change his perspective on black nationalism. Africans
in Algiers, Morocco, Arabia, Egypt, Iraq, and other parts of
the continent were Africans but not "Black" in the strict an-
thropological sense. Black nationalism as a political ideology

was separating Malcolm and his organization from millions of people in the Muslim world. To alleviate the ideological conflict, Malcolm advocated Pan-Africanism as the solution to the African-American problem. In Ghana, Malcolm talked to Dr. Kwame Nkrumah who " ... agreed that Pan-Africanism was the key also to the problems of those of African heritage."[24] Malcolm wanted to internationalize the plight of African-Americans. He was convinced of the inherent limitations of moral pressure and an "Americanized" struggle. Perceiving the race question as a domestic problem, leaders were limited to resolutions within the confines of United States, where blacks sought support from the same officials, organizations, and institutions that were oppressing them. Malcolm linked the African-American struggle with cultural and philosophical ties in Africa. Malcolm explained his Pan-African perspective as follows:

> It was time for all Afro-Americans to join the world's Pan-Africanist. Physically, we Afro-Americans might remain in America, fighting for our constitutional rights, but that philosophically and culturally we Afro-Americans badly needed to return to Africa and to develop a working unity in the framework of Pan-Africanism.[25]

Malcolm perceived the plight of the African American as similar to that of blacks in South Africa. The cross-cultural likeness of oppression qualified the United States' "race problem" as a denial of human rights and not merely a civil rights violation. Malcolm Shabazz wanted to present the cause of African Americans before the United Nations. Malcolm explained, " ... the American black man needed to recognize that he had a strong air-tight case to take the United States before the United Nations on a formal accusation of denial of human rights."[26] He went purely beyond a Pan-African perspective to include the Third World. He often spoke of Latin-American "brothers" and 800 million Chinese "brothers" supporting such a United Nations resolution. Minister Malcolm Shabazz did not live long enough to work toward these ideals.

On February 21, 1965, at 2:00 p.m., Malcolm Shabazz arrived at the Audubon Ballroom in New York City to speak to approximately 500 people. He greeted the audience with "Al-salaam alaikum" ("Peace be unto you"). "Wa-alaikum salaam" ("And unto you be peace"), answered the crowd. Then, in approximately the eighth row from the stage a fight started.

"Hold it! hold it! Don't get excited, " Malcolm pleaded.   Three
men in the front row stood and pointed guns at him and fired.
The bullets hit him in the head and chest with such force that
he was pushed over the chairs behind him.   Sixteen gunshot
pellets and revolver slugs dotted his shirt with blood.   Malcolm laid on the stage, his mouth wide open and his teeth
bared.   His wife, Betty Shabazz, pushed her way through the
crowd of people surrounding his body, fell to her knees,
grabbed his chest and cried, "They killed him. "   He was
rushed to the Vanderbilt Clinic one block away and at 3:00
p. m. , Minister El-Hajj Malik El Shabazz was pronounced
dead.

The autopsy performed by Dr. Milton Helper, Chief
Medical Examiner, revealed Shabazz died from shotgun wounds
in the heart, inflicted by a sawed-off shotgun, and he had
wounds from .45 and .38 caliber pistols.   Assistant Chief
Inspector Joseph Coyle, in charge of Manhattan North Detec-
tives, described the killing as a "well-planned conspiracy. "
Following Shabazz' assassination, three men were arrested
and accused of his murder: Talmadge Hayer, age 22; Thomas 15X Johnson, age 30; and Norman 3X Butler, age 26.

The three men charged with the murder of Minister
El-Hajj Malik El-Shabazz were former Muslims, which created
suspicion that the Nation of Islam had him killed.   Imam Wallace D. Muhammad felt the former Muslims were used: "I
don't believe that the Nation of Islam planned the assassination
of Malcolm X.   I believe outsiders assassinated Malcolm X
and members were used. "[27]

Talmadge Hayer admitted he purchased the guns (12-
gauge shot' gun, a .45 pistol, and a Luger) "hot" from the
street underworld.   Hayer and his colleagues investigated the
Audubon Ballroom on two occasions before the night Malcolm
was killed.   They attended one of Malcolm's rallies to see if
they would be searched.   He halted all searching of people
who attended his OAAU rallies because it reminded him too
much of Elijah Muhammad and the Nation of Islam.   He dismissed the search by saying, "If I can't be safe with my own
kind, where can I be?"   Hayer attended a dance on February
20, 1965, to observe the exits for escape routes.   The signal
for the murder to begin was when Malcolm greeted the audience with "Al-salaam alaikum. "   Initially Hayer refused to
say who his co-assassins were.   The police, equipped with
eyewitness descriptions of the assailants, arrested Johnson and
Butler because they matched the descriptions.   There was

such circumstantial evidence as their "strong man image" in
New York's Fruit of Islam. Also, both men were out on bail
for attempting to kill Benjamin Brown, who had defected from
the Nation of Islam and founded a rival organization in the
Bronx. Neither Johnson nor Butler confessed to killing Malcolm X; Hayer is the only confessed assassin and he impli-
cated the other two. The three men were sentenced to life
in prison. They were sent to Sing Sing and later shipped up-
state to Dannemora and maintained in solitary confinement.
For most of the 15 years of their incarceration, they had been
separated from each other--Hayer at Napanoch, Johnson at
Dannemora, and Butler at Sing Sing.

In autumn of 1977, Talmage Hayer confessed to Nur-
iddin Faiz, a Muslim prison chaplain, that he had lied and
Butler and Johnson were innocent. Hayer named four men
who were still active Muslims living in New Jersey. Faiz
contacted Defense Attorney William Kunstler, who agreed to
take the case for Johnson and Butler. Hayer supplied the
names, addresses, detailed descriptions, and occupations of
the four who, he now claimed, assisted him. Kunstler attempted to have the case reopened based upon Hayer's sworn
testimony.

In 1978, Kunstler was refused a new trial by Judge
Harold Rathway, who ruled Hayer's new testimony did not constitute enough evidence for another trial. The District Attorney's office of New York also resisted Attorney Kunstler's
legal pleas.

Kunstler petitioned the House of Representatives in the
spring of 1979 via the Congressional Black Caucus. The Black
Caucus was discussing the virtues and merits of Kunstler's
petitions. It was Attorney Kunstler's view that the Federal
Bureau of Investigation and the New York City police played
a supporting role in Malcolm's death. The FBI had Malcolm
and other leaders in the Nation of Islam under surveillance
for years as an "internal security risk" and also infiltrated
the organization with paid informants.

Hayer may have told the truth. Whoever killed Malcolm X, whether they were Muslims or agents of the state as
others have suggested, there are many riddles which remain
unsolved. Why weren't there searches at the door? Had Malcolm become so unrealistic that he thought his "own kind"
wouldn't attempt to kill him? Why did he refuse police protection? Why weren't the armed guards on stage? Why didn't

Malcolm arm himself? How could three members of the Nation of Islam as well-known as Hayer, Johnson, and Butler were to Malcolm and his organization slip into the room without being noticed? Many of these questions will go unanswered and we can only guess why Malcolm and his colleagues made such tragic mistakes.

There could have been inside help within Malcolm's organization to set him up which enabled the assassination to occur so smoothly. Many of the mistakes Malcolm made concerning his own personal security may relate to the drastic changes he had undergone during the year. Malcolm was fresh from the Hajj in Africa where he experienced genuine love and forgot that he may have been loved all over the world except in the United States. He had allowed himself the luxury of false consciousness concerning his security. Also, since he accepted Orthodox Islam, he might have assumed "Allah will protect me" and neglected to protect himself. It is ironic that El-Hajj Malik El-Shabazz made these fundamental errors because "Detroit Red" would have never allowed himself to be put in such a situation. Another ironic twist of Malcolm's murder is the fact that both he and his convicted assassins eventually moved away from Elijah Muhammad's doctrine and embraced Orthodox Islam. His assassins underwent a religious conversion in prison and now Talmage Hayer is called Majahid Abdul Halim, Norman Butler is Muhammad Abdul-Aziz, and Thomas 15X has changed his name to Khalil Islam.

We cannot say with any certainty where Malcolm was headed ideologically. His assassination put an abrupt halt to the process of redefining his perspective. It would be foolish to predict his direction and use it to support a specific ideology. It would be just as foolish not to use his life as a lesson, his leadership as an example, and his original approach to human rights to instruct others on their own development. He made enormous contributions to Pan-Africanism, as an advocate of human rights and toward efforts to acquire equality for people of African descent living in the United States. We have chronicled Malcolm's influence on the Nation of Islam. Many of the changes that were created in the Nation of Islam can directly be attributed to El-Hajj Malik El-Shabazz. Muhammad Akbar, a Muslim official, explains just one of his contributions:

> The primary influence in terms of changes was he foresaw the natural evolution of the movement. Malcolm saw the way Muslims were in the east. He

came back with the description of what was supposed to be an Islamic community. He visualized the ultimate form of the organization was more like the Orthodox Islamic world. "[28]

After the death of Malcolm Shabazz, his close friend Wallace D. Muhammad eventually succeeded his father, Elijah Muhammad. Wallace initiated many of the changes Malcolm had advocated. The following chapter will detail the alteration in the image and doctrine of the former Black Muslims to an Orthodox Islamic religious organization.

NOTES

1. Malcolm X, The Autobiography of Malcolm X (New York: Grove Press, 1964; New York: Ballantine Books, 1973, 1977), p. 10.

2. Ibid., p. 26.

3. Ibid., p. 73.

4. Ibid., p. 75.

5. Ibid., p. 290.

6. Interview, Imam Wallace D. Muhammad, Chicago, Illinois, July 25, 1979.

7. Ibid.

8. Malcolm X, Autobiography, pp. 241-242.

9. Ibid., p. 266.

10. Ibid., p. 265.

11. Ibid.

12. Ibid., p. 313.

13. Ibid., p. 299.

14. Ibid., p. 301.

15. Interview, Imam Wallace D. Muhammad.

16. Malcolm X, Autobiography, p. 301.

17. Ibid.

18. Ibid.

19. Ibid., p. 416.

20. Ibid., p. 375.

21. Pittsburgh Courier, March 6, 1965, p. 4.

22. Malcolm X, Autobiography, p. 375.

23. Ibid., p. 371.

24. Ibid., p. 357.

25. Ibid., p. 350.

26. Ibid., p. 361.

27. Interview, Imam Wallace D. Muhammad.

28. Interview, Muhammad Akbar, April 21, 1977.

Chapter VI

THE WORLD COMMUNITY OF AL-ISLAM IN THE WEST

> "The WCIW is an organized social movement and a religion but in line with the Koranic teachings. The old Nation of Islam was not in line with the Koranic teachings."
>
> --Imam Wallace D. Muhammad

After the assassination of Malcolm X, it was feared his death would be the catalyst for a "holy war" between the nationalists loyal to him and the followers of Elijah Muhammad who was placed under heavy guard in his Chicago residence. The Fruit of Islam and Chicago police officers kept the University of Islam and Muhammad Speaks newspaper under constant surveillance.

When Malcolm announced his split from the Nation of Islam on March 8, 1964, he began to build his organization until his death on February 21, 1965. One year was not enough time to establish a formal bureaucracy which would sustain his charisma and ideas after his death. One member of the OAAU expressed what most others felt, "He was the spirit, the force and the fiber of the movement; without him there is no movement."[1]

On February 23, 1965, in apparent retaliation for Malcolm's murder, the Harlem Mosque #7 at 102 W. 116th Street was fire-bombed; a Mosque in San Francisco was also fire-bombed. These two incidents created alarm that other acts of vengeance would follow.

Three days later, on February 26, 1965, the Nation of Islam held their annual Savior's Day Convention in Chicago. Elijah Muhammad blamed Malcolm's death on his departure from the Nation of Islam's doctrine saying, "We didn't want to kill Malcolm and we didn't try to. It was his foolishness, ignorance and his preachings that brought him to his death."[2]

During the convention, Malcolm's brothers, Wilfred and Philbert, refused to attend Malcolm's funeral services, denounced their brother for "going astray," and pledged their allegiance to Elijah Muhammad and the Nation of Islam.

Elijah Muhammad received additional support from his son Wallace D. Muhammad, who was accepted back into the organization during the Savior's Day Convention of 1965. Wallace returned to his father and asked for forgiveness. The reinstatement didn't last very long. Wallace said, "I was right back out. I was excommunicated three or four times and always for the same charge. I was not accepting the God image given to Fard Muhammad."[3]

After Wallace was suspended again in 1965, he remained inactive until he was readmitted in 1969. While he was suspended, the right to interact and communicate with members of his family was denied. During his suspension, he owned a bookstore and formed a study group called the Upliftment Society. Wallace also worked as a welder and operated a carpet and furniture cleaning business. He was accepted back into the organization in 1969 but did not regain his Mininster's status until 1974.

Entering the decade of the 1970's, the Nation of Islam continued to prosper in spite of the defections associated with Malcolm X, internal conflicts among the "royal family," and the deteriorating health of Elijah Muhammad. By the 1970's the organization grew to approximately one million members of which 250,000 are currently active.

Under Elijah Muhammad's leadership, the organization managed to acquire 15,000 acres of farmland in several states, thousands of head of cattle and sheep, poultry and dairy farms, warehouses and cold storage facilities, The Muhammad Speaks newspaper, tractor-trailer fleets, aircraft, The Guarranty Bank and Trust Company, apartment complexes, and wholesale and retail businesses throughout America. The Nation of Islam also managed to organize over seventy-six Muhammad Mosques of Islam in the United States and abroad in Bermuda,

Jamaica, Trinidad, Central America, England, Ghana, and the U.S. Virgin Islands. The Nation of Islam estimated that its business enterprises were valued at over $85,000,000 by the late 1970's.

In 1974, Wallace D. Muhammad was accepted back into the ministry and assumed authority over the Chicago Mosque. Wallace was given complete freedom to preach as his wisdom dictated. He said, "I would actually test the support for me from the Honorable Elijah Muhammad. I would say things that I knew were different than some of the things taught under his leadership."[4]

Wallace and his father repeatedly engaged in ideological conflicts for over 14 years. Finally, in 1974, Elijah Muhammad gave his consent to relinquish the "Black Muslims" doctrine for the Orthodox model presented by Wallace.

One fateful afternoon in 1974, officers of the Fruit of Islam brought a recording of one of Wallace's sermons to Elijah Muhammad; he summoned Wallace to listen with him. At one point during the recording Elijah Muhammad exclaimed, "My son's got it, my son can go anywhere on earth and preach."[5] With those words, uttered before Muslim officials, Elijah began the transfer of power. Before the transfer was complete, he became seriously ill.

On January 29, 1975, Elijah Muhammad was admitted to Chicago's Mercy Hospital for a routine medical examination. On February 8, 1975, he was rushed into the intensive care unit after he was stricken with congestive heart failure. His condition continued to deteriorate. At 8:10 a.m. on February 25, 1975, he was pronounced dead by his physician, Dr. Charles Williams.

On February 26, 1975, at the annual Savior's Day Rally before 20,000 members and friends of the organization, Abass Rassoull, National Secretary of the Nation of Islam, announced that Wallace D. Muhammad was chosen to lead the Nation of Islam. The appointment of Wallace D. Muhammad astonished the general public because he had kept a relatively low profile up to that point. However, members of the Nation of Islam knew as early as 1958 that Wallace would succeed his father.

Wallace D. Muhammad was born in Detroit, Michigan, on October 30, 1933. He received his entire elementary and high school education at the University of Islam in Chicago.

He studied microbiology, English, history, and social sciences
at Wilson and Loop Junior College in Chicago. He has been
employed as a painter, carpet cleaner, grocery store and
restaurant manager, and welder for U. S. Steel and Bethlehem
Steel. He has operated his own bookstore and served as a
lieutenant in the Fruit of Islam. In 1967, Wallace made a
pilgrimage to Mecca and later two umaras (out-of-season pilgrimage). He was the minister of the Philadelphia Temple
for three years, from 1958 to 1961. He was sentenced to
three years in the Sandstone Minnesota Federal Correctional
Institution for failing to report to Elgin State Hospital as required under the laws affecting conscientious objectors.

Why was Wallace D. Muhammad selected to lead and
not other members of the organization? The family of Elijah Muhammad was known as the "Royal Family" among members of the organization. Only members of the family could
succeed Elijah Muhammad.

Wallace D. Muhammad was "chosen for the mission."
He was chosen to succeed his father by Wali Fard Muhammad,
who told Elijah that his seventh child would be a son and his
eventual successor. "This new-born baby predicted by Fard
Muhammad that [sic] he would be a male and it so happened
the guess was right."[6]

The seventh child was a son and Elijah Muhammad
named him Wallace D. Muhammad in honor of Wali Fard, the
founder of the Nation of Islam. Imam Wallace D. Muhammad
explained why he was chosen to lead, "I was chosen because
a new baby, new birth--they wanted a Christ figure, someone
with a mystery about [him]."[7]

With the death of Elijah Muhammad, Wallace was free
to shape the movement as he saw fit. Elijah Muhammad's
passing brought to an end the bulwark of black separatism,
black identity and consciousness in the United States.

Through the reorganizing, denationalizing, decentralizing
and orthodoxing of the Nation of Islam into the World Community of Al-Islam in the West, Wallace D. Muhammad has
changed the most powerful and feared black nationalist group
into an Orthodox Islamic religion. He said he is changing the
religion, " ... in a way which will gain acceptance in America; this is the kind of thinking I have to encourage in our
membership."[8]

Wallace D. Muhammad engineered a series of conceptual changes which altered the character and structure of the Nation of Islam. He debunked the racial superiority doctrine of Elijah Muhammad; redefined Wali Fard Muhammad as a wise man instead of "God in person"; restored Malcolm X to a position of respect and prominence in the organization; separated business from religious practices; ceased the demand for a separate state; began to honor the American Constitution, and brought the doctrine in line with Orthodox Islamic practices.

One of the first official acts of Imam Wallace D. Muhammad's administration was to reinterpret his father's role as "Messenger of Allah." Wallace felt his father had not been speaking in the theological spirit of the Koran and the Bible. Instead, he felt his father had been saying of Wali Fard "A man came to me with solutions for your health problems, social problems and I am bringing you the message he gave to me."[9]

Imam Wallace D. Muhammad often read Fard's doctrine and therefore knew Elijah Muhammad was the person who defined Fard as God in person. Fard referred to himself as a messenger of God and Elijah Muhammad reinterpreted his message.

Wallace D. Muhammad redefined both men's contributions to the organization. Wali Fard is now recognized as the founder of the movement and not "God in person," as Elijah Muhammad had suggested. To coincide with Orthodox Islam, Wallace D. Muhammad defines "Allah as a supernatural being that acts out his wishes through his vessels on earth, those who submit to Allah."[10]

Elijah Muhammad believed African Americans were Asiatic descendants from the tribe of Shabazz. Wallace D. Muhammad has changed the Asiatic nationality to the term "Bilalians." Bilal was an Ethiopian Muslim who was born circa A.D. 600. Bilal was so firm in his convictions that when punished by the slave master after refusing to denounce Islam, he would cry, "Ahad! Ahad!" ("One, only one God").

By changing the name of their nationality, Wallace D. Muhammad created a spiritual and national bond with Islam as a religion and Africa as a continent. They have a double connection with Bilal because he was a Muslim and he was also a so-called African."[11] The Muhammad Speaks news-

paper was renamed the Bilalian News, effective November 1,
1975.

Another alteration in organization policy occurred when
the organization changed its belief in the inherent evil of white
people. Islam does not restrict its membership to one race
nor does it advocate racial superiority. The racial doctrine
that depicted whites as devils has been changed to describe
a devil mentality, which motivates individuals to commit evil
deeds. Blacks as well as whites can be affected by a devil
mentality. Minister Abdul Haleem Farrakhan explains the new
doctrine: "What Honorable Elijah Muhammad gave us in physical terms had spiritual meaning. They didn't graft him physically [Yacub's creation of whites] but it's a mentality. There
is no devil just limited to white flesh."[12]

For several years Elijah Muhammad advocated that the
United States government should give the Nation of Islam several states to create a separate nation. It was Elijah Muhammad's belief that Muslims were not really citizens of the
United States because blacks were not given the privileges
associated with citizenship status. Discrimination in employment, education, and housing denied blacks the opportunity to
fully participate in the society. Until social economic conditions
were changed, members of the Nation of Islam did not vote,
run for office, or join the military.

Wallace D. Muhammad felt it was futile to demand a
separate state within the United States. Keeping his vow to
Islam acceptable to the government and society at large and
to enhance its image, he encouraged Muslims to honor the
American flag and urged members to vote. He explained,
"As citizens of the United States of America we are obligated
to defend the USA. But if you yourself think it is wrong to go
to war, that's between you and God."[13]

It was inevitable that Wallace D. Muhammad would re-
store Malcolm X Shabazz to a place of honor within the organization. Malcolm was instrumental in the development of
the movement in his Prime Minister role for Elijah Muhammad. His charisma, recruitment efforts, and organizational
skills helped propel the Nation of Islam from an obscure local
sect to a powerful religious organization with international
connections. Many of the present members agreed with Malcolm's view of an Islamic community. Wallace reiterated this
point: "Many people agreed with the stand Malcolm took but
remained in the Nation of Islam. Although Malcolm left the

Nation of Islam, I'm glad he remained a Muslim."[14]   Malcolm
and Wallace were close friends and they were both excommunicated by Elijah Muhammad almost simultaneously.   Malcolm
and Wallace maintained their friendship while exiled from the
Nation of Islam.   To respect his contribution to the development of the organization, the New York City Mosque was
named Malcolm Shabazz Mosque # 7.

Wallace D. Muhammad has also changed the rituals and
dress of the membership and the decor of the buildings.
Mosques are now referred to as "Masjids" and instead of anti-
American, anti-Christian slogans on the walls, there are Arabic symbols.   Tape-recorded sounds of Eastern music and
Islamic prayers filter throughout the Masjid.   People are no
longer searched, but must leave their shoes at the front door.
Seats have been replaced by carpet and everyone sits on the
floor, although the seating is still segregated by sex.   All
adult males sit in the front, the young boys sit behind the
men, followed by the women and girls.   During services a
local Imam leads the congregation in a prayer.

The worshipers are asked to stand facing the east with
cupped hands before them and bowed heads while the minister
prays in Arabic and then in English.   The membership also
believes in the two basic faiths of Islam: belief in the oneness
of God and that Muhammad is the messenger and prophet of
Allah.

WCIW also practices the devotional duties, or pillars
of Islam (testimony, prayer, fasting, alms, and pilgrimage).
Wallace D. Muhammad has brought the religious beliefs, rituals, and practices in line with Orthodox Islam.

Under Elijah Muhammad's leadership, there had been
a strict dress and grooming code.   Wallace D. Muhammad
allows the members to wear anything they want so long as it
is neat, clean, and does not degrade the religion.   Women
are allowed to wear pants and do not have to cover their heads
except while attending Muslim functions.   Muslim ministers,
or Imams, often wear Eastern-style leisure suits with a high
collar buttoned at the neck.   National Spokesman, Louis Farrakhan, explained the change as an emphasis on uniformity of
mind, not dress: "The Honorable Elijah Muhammad was building us towards not a uniform dress but a uniformity of mind.
And once we have uniformity of mind, we can dress any way
that mind directs us."[15]

Women in the Nation of Islam under the administration

of Elijah Muhammad had a subordinate role to men. Wallace
D. Muhammad has changed that role, and in many cases wom-
en are placed over men in administrative positions.

There is also a change in the nature of the Muslim
girls' training and general civilization class. Traditionally,
the classes taught " ... the basic principles of keeping the
house, taking care of children and taking care of her husband."16 The class has been changed in name and substance,
according to Sharon Shabazz. "The Muslim Women's Development Class, established by Wallace Muhammad, looks at life
in a broader sense. She is encouraged as a woman to fulfill
her mental capabilities."17

Wallace D. Muhammad studied the role of women during
the early development of Islam; he believes the right of women
to equal education is protected under Islamic law. Wallace
justifies the new status by saying, "We cannot make any dis-
tinctions between men and women in terms of intelligence,
spirituality or moral nature. Women are equal with men and
they are not to be treated any differently."18

Under Elijah Muhammad, the organization managed
numerous businesses. Wallace D. Muhammad has separated
the spiritual from the business element of the organization.
He has liquidated more than $6 million in long-term debts
and tax obligations and has sold less profitable enterprises.

The business ventures were managed by ministers of
local Masjids who also had religious duties to fulfill. Farms
and other property have been leased to Muslims and non-
Muslims. Wallace D. Muhammad explained the arrangement:
" ... these individuals have a freehand to manage the income,
monies and operation. We just look for him to show a profit.
If he shows a profit, we want our share."19

By adhering to Orthodox Islam, there are economic and
political benefits as well as spiritual ones. If Wallace D. Muhammad had followed his father's doctrine, the organization
would still be alienated from the international Islamic community. The changes began to bear fruit early during Wallace's
administration.

Egyptian President, Anwar El Sadat, arrived in Wash-
inton, D.C. on October 26, 1975. After his visit with President Ford, he traveled to Chicago where he had a private
session with Imam Wallace D. Muhammad in Sadat's hotel

suite in the Drake Hotel. The Egyptian government awarded
the WCIW twelve scholarships to enable Muslim students to
attend Egyptian universities.

During an interview Imam Wallace D. Muhammad was
asked his opinion of the proposed peace agreement between
Egypt and Israel. He replied, "The Islamic world leadership
has much to gain from the political psychology of President
Sadat. He is inviting his people to come away from an emotional response to the presence of Israel on Muslim land to
a more philosophical, rational strategy."[20]

The change in doctrine has also made the organization
more compatible with the government of the United States. In
February 1979, the WCIW was awarded $22 million (the larg-
est amount ever awarded to a black firm) by the Department
of Commerce. The WCIW, in conjunction with American
Pouch Foods Company, is producing precooked combat rations
for the United States military. The contract will provide 400
jobs for Chicago residents.

Certain segments of the organization have resisted Wallace D. Muhammad's changes. The most significant development is the defection of International Spokesman, Louis Abdul
Farrakhan, who announced his departure in December 1977.
Farrakhan disagreed with many changes initiated by Wallace
and continues to follow the doctrine of Elijah Muhammad. Farrakhan felt the move to Orthodox Islam has caused a decrease
in financial holdings and created a lack of discipline among
the members. Farrakhan has formed another organization
(the Nation of Islam) based upon the doctrine of Elijah Muhammad.

Louis Abdul Farrakhan publishes the newspaper The
Final Call, which features Elijah Muhammad's picture and the
traditional "wants and beliefs" which comprise the program of
the Nation of Islam. Farrakhan also sells publications written
by Elijah Muhammad and refers to himself as "Elijah Muhammad's national representative."

Wallace D. Muhammad perceives Farrakhan's organization as political and not religious. He says, "I think he is
trying to stay abreast politically with the Black Movement.
Farrakhan has ability and intelligence to speak and deal with
the African problem in the context of man's problem on earth."[21]

The WCIW is comprised of 138 Masjids domestically

TABLE VII

WORLD COMMUNITY OF AL-ISLAM IN THE WEST ORGANIZATIONAL STRUCTURE

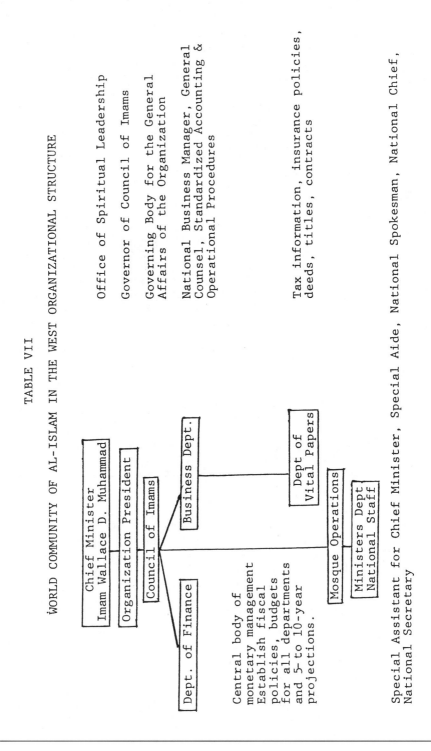

Chief Minister Imam Wallace D. Muhammad	
Organization President	
Council of Imams	
Office of Spiritual Leadership	
Governor of Council of Imams	
Governing Body for the General Affairs of the Organization	

Business Dept. — National Business Manager, General Counsel, Standardized Accounting & Operational Procedures

Dept of Vital Papers — Tax information, insurance policies, deeds, titles, contracts

Dept. of Finance — Central body of monetary management. Establish fiscal policies, budgets for all departments and 5- to 10-year projections.

Mosque Operations

Ministers Dept National Staff

Special Assistant for Chief Minister, Special Aide, National Spokesman, National Chief, National Secretary

TABLE VII (Continued)

Muslim Women's Development Class Director, Minister of Justice, Assistant Minister of Education, Consultants on National Education Staff

Serves as representative of all the Mosque Communities established throughout the country

Acts as a liaison between the Nation of Islam and the Mosque is established in the community

```
                    National Steering Committee
                              |
                         Committees
       _____|_____
      |            |           |           |            |
  Ways &       Child        Sick      Accident      Creation    Fairness
  Means       Interest                & Mishap
```

```
Censor Board          Public
for Cultural          Information
Development
```

```
                 Dept. of Human Affairs
      _____|_____
     |                  |                  |
Human Development   Human Relations    Dept. of Community
    Staff              Staff              Services
```

and internationally (Jamaica, Bahamas, Bermuda, and Barbados). The Masjid represents the basic organization unit in the WCIW. The most important rank in each Masjid is the Imam (Minister). Imam Muhammad Akbar explains the change in the structure under Wallace D. Muhammad as " ... removal of autocratic centralized leadership of the organization. A shift to a more democratic and shared decision-making process. That has been the most radical change in the organization."[22] Under Elijah Muhammad, all power was centralized in Chicago; local Masjids had very little autonomy. (See Table VII on pages 98-99 for a complete breakdown of WCIW's organizational structure.)

On September 12, 1978, Wallace D. Muhammad announced his resignation as spiritual leader of the organization to become an evangelist or ambassador-at-large. He now speaks on behalf of the organization domestically and internationally. The governing of the organization is being administered by a council of six Imams. Each member has equal power nationally, but total power in his respective region; each Imam serves a one-year term. The Imams on the council in 1980 were Ali Rahid, New York City; Khalil Abdel Alim, Washington, D.C.; James Shabazz, Chicago; Ibrahim Kamel Udein, Houston; Ibrahim Pusha, Atlanta; and Karim Hasan, Los Angeles.

Wallace D. Muhammad provided 17 nominations and the group's membership voted for six via telephone hook-up. He requested the council to adhere to the teachings of the Koran, to become actively involved in the capitalistic system and committed to the government of the United States, and to maintain a position of neutrality on affairs of Arab nations. Wallace D. Muhammad, as ambassador-at-large will be involved in public speaking and interviews to make the public more knowledgeable of the organization.

When Imam Wallace D. Muhammad was asked why he chose to fulfill the role of ambassador-at-large, he replied:

> I was not satisfied with the response in the ministerial body to my call for us to get out in the broader community and let our contributions be known. We are fighting the same evils that Christians are fighting. In fact, I have spoken outside the community more than I have spoken inside. [23]

Wallace, in his role as spiritual leader, has managed

to alter the doctrine, character, and direction of the former "Black Muslims." These changes enabled the World Community of Al-Islam in the West to be accepted by the Islamic World Community and also be accepted by the United States government. The organization is no longer considered a threat to internal security.

The transformation of the organization has been a reflection of the leadership during various stages of development. Wali Fard founded the organization during the Depression and Elijah Muhammad skillfully maneuvered the Nation of Islam into a position to aid the African-American communities. The organization might still be a separatist movement without the influence of Malcolm X Shabazz on Wallace D. Muhammad and the entire Muslim community. Wallace's ideological struggles with his father ultimately led to the creation of the World Community of Al-Islam in the West. It is too early to predict if the changes will be beneficial. The WCIW is working toward an "accepted religion" status.

The majority of black people are still deprived of basic political-economic necessities. The same social problems the Nation of Islam tried to cure still exist. The WCIW is taking a different approach to remedy the social ills faced by millions of Americans.

NOTES

1. New York Post, February 23, 1965.

2. New York Post, February 28, 1965.

3. Interview, Imam Wallace D. Muhammad, Chicago, Illinois, July 25, 1979.

4. Ibid.

5. Ibid.

6. Ibid.

7. Ibid.

8. Ibid.

9. Ibid.

10. Public Address, Imam Wallace D. Muhammad, Richmond, Virginia, April 1, 1977.

11. Bilalian News, October 24, 1976, p. 31.

12. Public Address, Louis Farrakhan, Richmond, Virginia, February 4, 1976.

13. Public Address, Imam Wallace D. Muhammad.

14. Ibid.

15. Public Address, Louis Farrakhan.

16. Interview, Sharon Shabazz, New York City, New York, December 16, 1975.

17. Ibid.

18. Interview, Imam Wallace D. Muhammad.

19. Ibid.

20. Ibid.

21. Ibid.

22. Interview (telephone), Muhammad Akbar, Chicago, Illinois, April 21, 1977.

23. Interview, Imam Wallace D. Muhammad.

For 45 years the Nation of Islam was the most significant
black separatist organization in the United States. The organization combined an economic program to uplift the masses,
black pride through identification with ancient and contemporary
African societies, and separatism as the solution to economic
inequality and racism in the United States. Blyden, Garvey,
and Drew Ali had propagated similar ideologies previously.
However, the Nation of Islam overshadows previous organizations because of its longevity and programs that affect thousands of people throughout the United States and abroad.

There is no doubt that the Nation of Islam was a movement of the masses. In the urban ghettos, clean-shaven, bow
tie-wearing Muslims were often on the streets where members
of traditional religious bodies feared to tread. The outreach
program enabled Muslims to work among the people, selling
fish, the Muhammad Speaks newspaper, and organizing.
Whether one agreed with their doctrine or not, their record
of community development was unmatched.

The Nation of Islam managed to survive attacks by the
FBI in addition to being subject to infiltration and other unethical behavior. Established churches and civil rights leaders, fearful of losing government and white support, avoided
the Nation of Islam as if it were a colony of lepers.

The Nation of Islam was essentially Elijah Muhammad's
organization. He was a remarkable human being. Here was
a man with a fourth grade education, who was short on charisma but possessed an enormous amount of fortitude and dedication to the cause. He migrated to Detroit from Georgia in
1923, but became disillusioned by the "promised land" and
joined the Nation of Islam. When Fard Muhammad left the

movement, Elijah Muhammad guided the organization through
turbulant conditions for over forty years.   Men with more
education and charisma looked up to and admired him; his
authority was rarely questioned.

The fact that the organization was not purely Islamic
does not tarnish the reality of the Nation of Islam having been
an important vehicle for social change.   Many black people
did not adhere to the organization's beliefs, but the Nation of
Islam did raise their consciousness of African heritage and
provided jobs for many inner-city residents.

Many leaders, both black and white, do not want to
accept or admit that the black minority may not achieve equality under the present economic order and political system.
Elijah Muhammad felt a separate state was the only solution to
the problem.   The Nation of Islam had three alternatives;
either change the society (acquire a separate state), continue
to advocate for separation, or alter its doctrine to become
compatible with the government of the United States.   Obviously, the current leadership has accepted the last alternative.
Now the World Community of Al-Islam in the West is praised
by civic, government, and religious leaders.   They have contracts with the United States government and often hold functions in conjunction with Christian organizations.

Whether one agrees or not with the changes Wallace
D. Muhammad has made, he had the right to change.   Members of the organization say Elijah Muhammad himself accepted the changes as the fulfillment of his own mission.   Wallace is a deeply religious man, devoted to the cause of Islam.
He is guided by his knowledge of the Koran and belief in Allah.   Whether the WCIW will prosper or not is too early to
predict.   History will record their achievements and generations yet to be born will judge their contribution.   However,
there are two facts that cannot be debated: it is no longer a
black separatist movement nor are its members Black Muslims.   The World Community of Al-Islam in the West is comprised of Muslims who believe in Islam.   The transition from
Black Muslims to Muslims is complete.

Appendix

INTERVIEW WITH IMAM
WALLACE D. MUHAMMAD

The Chief Minister of the World Community of
Al-Islam in the West, Imam Wallace D. Muhammad, was interviewed by the author in Chicago
on July 25, 1979.

CEM: Was the Nation of Islam (NOI) a social movement organization or a religion?

WDM: It was a religion and a social movement organization. In fact, the religion as it was introduced
to the Nation of Islam was more a social reform philosophy than Orthodox Islam.

CEM: How would you define the World Community
of Al-Islam in the West?

WDM: A combination of both, but in line with the
Koranic teachings. The old organization teachings
were not in line with the Koranic teachings.

CEM: Were social and economic conditions during
the thirties instrumental in the development of the
ideology?

WDM: They certainly were. I think the present community thinking in the World Community of Al-Islam
in the West is a result of the earlier teachings. We
find many Islamic organizations but I don't believe

there is one to be found like ours. I don't
know of a single Islamic organization in America or outside that is really like ours. We
put emphasis on the application of religion in one's
daily life and involvement in the outer community.
In the East, Muslims do apply their religion to their
daily lives because that's what it's for. But few of
them who live in America practice their religion that
way.

As you know, we are addressing community issues
and are trying to find some common ground for Muslims and non-Muslims. The old Nation of Islam was
designed to fight problems peculiar to black people--
social problems, lack of economic development among
poor blacks, and alcoholism. In those days, dope
addiction wasn't much of a problem. Alcoholism was
treated. The earlier teachings were designed to give
us a socialism ideology. In fact, it did introduce a
socialist philosophy. That's why it was feared in the
earlier days, the early thirties.

The members were locked up in Chicago and Detroit in the middle thirties. The original teacher who
introduced the NOI was ordered out of Detroit. Then
he came to Chicago in 1934--within months [he] was
asked to leave Chicago. He left the movement. The
pressure on the Nation of Islam during its early development was out of fear of a kind of Communist
philosophy being introduced in the guise of religion.

CEM: Was Marcus Garvey's Black Factories Corporation influential in the Honorable Elijah Muhammad's
creation of the business enterprises?

WDM: Not only the Honorable Elijah Muhammad, but
his teacher who was a foreigner and not an American,
Fard Muhammad [was also influenced by Garvey].
His teachings was obviously influenced by Garvey and
Noble Drew Ali, who started the Moorish America
movement. I say that because the dress he originally
gave the male members of the Fruit of Islam is the
same dress the Drew Ali people had. The garbs the
women wore were like the garbs the Marcus Garvey
women wore. The emphasis on identity, black identity,
and economic development--I am sure that was influenced by the Garvey teachings.

CEM: Was Wallace Fard Muhammad ever a member

of the Moorish Science Temple, or did he just study the teachings of Noble Drew Ali?

WDM: I don't believe he was ever a member. He was really a very wise man in Islamic teachings and comparative religion, very wise in understanding the symbolisms in religion. I think what he did was to look for a way to introduce the Koran in the black community. He studied Noble Drew Ali's approach. I believe he felt that Drew Ali had that as a part of his own plan. His own plan was to introduce the Koran but he didn't; he produced a small booklet that he called "Koran," but it had no resemblance to the Koran at all.

Professor Fard introduced the whole text of the Koran--the complete text as it is known all over the world--to the Nation of Islam. To introduce it he had to put it in the package of Drew Ali. The teachings he gave us were very similar to what Drew Ali gave his people. He taught us we were black Asiatics and descendants of a great Islamic Kingdom; Drew Ali taught his people the same. He taught us the Caucasians were devils and Drew Ali taught his people the same. A lot of his people don't know this. He identified white people with the embodiment of evil in scripture, which is Satan. But he was more elusive than Fard Muhammad was. Drew Ali said white people were the rider of the horse--he took that out of the Bible to identify the white man as the pale horse, whose rider is death. He didn't say devil, but the angel of death riding a pale horse is disguised as the devil. Fard Muhammad, because of his comparative religious studies, was able to pick up what the average follower of Drew Ali couldn't pick up--Caucasian race is the embodiment of evil. Fard Muhammad came out in plain language and said they are devils.

CEM: What is the status of the numerous business enterprises since your administration? Does the World Community of Al-Islam in the West still run and control the enterprises?

WDM: Well, no. I couldn't say we do. We leave it to individuals and corporations that are formed within WCIW and some without. We have a property manager now ... Brother Omar. He manages prop-

erties and he is independent. If we have a complaint,
it's like the tenant giving the landlord a complaint.
He has a free hand to manage the income, monies,
and everything. We just look for him to show a profit. If he shows a profit we want our share. He
runs the management of the real estate. What used
to be Salaam Restaurant is now in the hands of another brother, Brother Omar. The farms that used
to be operated by members in the community are now
leased out to others, to outsiders.

CEM: You have established Masjids in several Caribbean locations,   Barbados, Bermuda, Jamiaca,
Nassau-Bahamas, St. Thomas and St. Croix, V. I.
Why have you established Masjids in the Caribbean
and what role do you see the West Indians playing in
the struggle for human rights?

WDM: I have a personal interest in the Caribbean,
but it was not my personal interest that brought about
the establishment of Masjids in the Caribbean.   They
were actually established under the Honorable Elijah
Muhammad.   What we did was try to improve the
membership and propagation work.

CEM: Could you tell me something about Fard Muhammad's background and why he disappeared so mysteriously?

WDM: I believe he was a genius of theology, with
reference to its symbolic nature.   The really inter-
esting thing about Fard Muhammad--which Elijah Muhammad himself recognized--is that this man was
introducing himself as a Christ figure to displace the
"old" Christ that Christianity gave black people.
That is what caused him to disappear so mysteriously;
he wanted to create mystery about himself.
    A number of things he did ... [were] mere cheap
magic or premature witch doctor's tricks.   The Honorable Elijah Muhammad used to talk about how he
took a strand of his hair out of his head and told
some of the members to take a strand of hair from
their heads.   They would all put the hairs in one
pile and Fard Muhammad would take a strand from
his head and lift them all up.   The Honorable Elijah
Muhammad, being the son of a Baptist preacher who
had preached for fifty years, made the connection

Imam Wallace D. Muhammad (right) and Clifton E. Marsh

right away, "Lift me up and I will draw all men unto
me!" They tell me Fard Muhammad would come
one day and his hair would be completely gray and
he would appear the next time and--no gray hair.
He purposely tried to draw their attention.

CEM: You have stated that you were chosen for the
mission to lead. Why were you selected to replace
the Honorable Elijah Muhammad and not other members of your family and/or other members of the
organization?

WDM: The power of mystery. The other children
were already born when Fard Muhammad came. I
was the only child born during his stay with us. I
was chosen because a new baby, new birth--they
wanted a Christ figure, someone with a mystery
about [him]. Here was this newborn baby predicted
by Fard Muhammad to be a male and it so happened
the guess was right. I say a "guess" not to laugh
at our religion. I say "guess" because that's the
language the Honorable Elijah Muhammad used.

WDM: I hope I represent the Honorable Elijah Muhammad.   To me the Honorable Elijah Muhammad
was a man like I try to be.   That is, a wise leader
for his people.   He was a man that laughed and joked,
but he was very serious, even his jokes were serious, even his jokes were a teaching.   I have admired
his wisdom and I try to follow it.

CEM: You have decentralized the organization, where
is the central leadership of the organization now?

WDM: The central leadership is still in myself, but
it's not an absolute leadership.   The power is shared
with a council of Imams and about 17 advisors to that
council.   Many others not named [are] in the body of
advisors.   We try to share the leadership.   The
Imams' meeting going on right now is supervised by
Brother Imam Fatah; he has a free hand to do that.
The business, real estate, and other capital holdings
throughout the country--we look to the people who
are over those regions to make the best decisions
for the interest of the community.

CEM: Detroit is presently the Midwest regional

Imam Wallace D. Muhammad

headquarters?

WDM: Yes it is.   Dr. G. Haleen Shabazz is the
Imam over the Midwest region.

CEM: What is the status of Muhammad Ali in the
organization now?

WDM: Actually, his membership, in my opinion,
is an honorary one.

CEM: What does that mean?

WDM: That means we hardly ever see him, but we
still honor his membership.

CEM: Why did Louis Farrakhan leave the World
Community of Al-Islam in the West and what is he
doing now?

WDM: To my knowledge, he is preaching a kind of
moderate form of the very early teachings.   I'd say
he has gone back in time; he has gone back further
than the Honorable Elijah Muhammad himself was at
the time of his death.   To try to introduce again,
black nationalist philosophy, I think he is trying to
stay abreast politically with the black movement.
     In my opinion, he is doing a disservice to him-
self.   He has ability, intelligence to deal with the
African problem in the context of man's problems
on earth.   That's the only way to deal with it, in my
opinion.

CEM: You originally had a national decision-making
board.   Has that been disbanded in favor of the Council?

WDM: We had a decision-making board.   The name
itself created a problem--the name of the board.   I
was the Chief Administrator over the board.   The
old habit of passing the buck gave that structure too
many problems.   The council of Imams didn't replace
that body but we have found leadership to satisfy us.
Whereas, with the decision-making board we did not
have the leadership to satisfy us.

CEM: Malcolm X Shabazz was suspended from the

Nation of Islam in 1964. The same year you and
your brother Akbar left the movement. Was there
any relationship between the two events?

WDM: Yes.   When Minister Malcolm was suspended
I was already excommunicated.   I was the first to
be excommunicated.   Then Minister Malcolm received
the suspension.   When Minister Malcolm received the
suspension, it was news right away, but because of
my low profile and almost insignificant position in
the Nation of Islam at that time, the news of my suspension did not hit the press like Malcolm's suspension did.
     I was charged with trying to influence Malcolm's
theological thinking.   I was also charged with giving
him personal, private knowledge of the Honorable
Elijah Muhammad's living, which was a lie.   I told
him at the time I was falsely accused and I would
like to face the accusers.   The Honorable Elijah Muhammad told me, "Malcolm X is not facing his accusers either.   We're talking to you separately."
So he talked to me separately and he made his decision right there.   His decision was to excommunicate
me.

CEM: How did you influence Malcolm X's theological
thinking?

WDM: I have no knowledge of any effort on my part
to influence his theological thinking.   That was the
accusation made.   Malcolm X ... said I had been an
influence in his life.   He didn't put it that way but
in effect that's what he said.   I had been an influence
on his religious thinking, second to the Honorable
Elijah Muhammad.

CEM: What year were you excommunicated?

WDM: The first time must have been late 1964.

CEM: You say the first time; you were excommunicated twice?

WDM: No.   Many times--at least three or four times
and always for the same charge that I was not accepting the God-image given to Fard Muhammad.

CEM: What was the longest period you were suspended and what did you do during your suspension?

WDM: The longest period of my suspension was between the years 1964 and 1969.   During that time I was stripped of all minister's privileges.   In 1966, early 1967 all support--even family relations were denied me.   I couldn't even socialize with family members.   During this period I had several jobs. First, I bought a carpet and furniture cleaning machine and started cleaning carpet and furniture just on my own.   It was very hard.   I didn't have enough money to run an office.   I couldn't advertise; I just had to go from customer to customer.   I did manage to live and finally I got a good welding job and things improved for me.

CEM: You were admitted back into the organization in 1969?

WDM: No.   I don't believe it was '69.   In '69 things began to warm up.   In 1970 I was admitted back. Once right after Malcolm's assassination I was admitted back, but that didn't last very long.   I was right back out.   I was admitted back in 1970 again. I stayed in the good graces of Elijah Muhammad until now.

CEM: When did the changes start to take place in the organization?   I am sure it didn't occur in 1975. Did you start discussing the transformation long before then?

WDM: No.   Not long before then.   I would say nine months to a year.   It was in 1974 that the Honorable Elijah Muhammad accepted me back into the ministry. I started teaching here in Chicago.   The Honorable Elijah Muhammad gave me complete freedom to teach here in Chicago with Imam Shaw.   At one point he told me to assume authority of the Mosque here in Chicago.   From that point on I was free to propagate and preach as my own wisdom dictated.   I say that because I would actually test the support for me from the Honorable Elijah Muhammad.   Nobody else was restricting my movement; I answered only to the Honorable Elijah Muhammad.   I would say things I know were different from some of the things the people had been taught under the leadership of Elijah Muhammad. I would use my own discretion. I would test what the Honorable Elijah Muhammad would accept. He never ever called me in and said what I was teaching was causing problems [or to] slow up or go in another direction. He was satisfied with it.

One time a tape was brought to the Honorable Elijah Muhammad by officers of the FOI [Fruit of Islam], who were like the police in the Nation of Islam, checking everything. He hadn't heard it himself. He called me over and played it while I was present.... He jumped up out of his seat and applauded and said, "My son's got it!" That's what he told the officers sitting around the table and his wife. He said, "My son can go anywhere on earth and preach."

CEM: The Pillars of Islam include testimony, prayer, fasting, alms, and pilgrimage to Mecca. Did the Nation of Islam follow these principles and does the World Community of Al-Islam in the West follow them?

WDM: We follow them. The Nation of Islam accepted those principles. They were vaguely taught; they weren't clearly taught. Fasting was taught. We fasted during December; we didn't fast during the proper month. The Honorable Elijah Muhammad didn't bother with that. He picked December. He explains the reasons for picking December, because during that time you are normally converted to Christian life. You have a tendency to go out and waste your money and get into the Christmas season. So we used this month because it's good protection for us. He introduced December as the month of Ramadan, which is unorthodox Islam. During the last four or five years of his life, he began to observe the month of Ramadan in the Islamic calendar.

CEM: Under Elijah Muhammad, members were discouraged from serving in the armed services, voting or supporting political candidates. Why? And have you changed this?

WDM: Minister Malcolm, in his attack on the conservative leadership when he was suspended, described the Nation of Islam as a straitjacket religion. I

don't take too well to that kind of criticism but I
think Malcolm X had discovered something. He was
very emphatic and clear in what he had to say. He
didn't beat around the bush. The Honorable Elijah
Muhammad admitted he was containing our minds to
remake our minds. He said, "If I let you go out
into the world, you will never become the people
Allah wants you to be." He designed the teachings
to contain the thinking of his followers. While he
was containing their thinking, it was almost as if he
had their brains on a lab table. He was treating
social diseases, operating on their minds. This kind
of containment of the thinking of the people didn't
allow the Honorable Elijah Muhammad to introduce
new concepts to his people. The concepts remained
mystical, and even fictional ... many concepts of
the religion as the birth of God. The Christians
don't have a concept like that. They say the birth
of Jesus but not the birth of God.

CEM: Three of the basic principles of the Nation of
Islam were Wallace Fard Muhammad is God, the
white man is the devil, and Elijah Muhammad is the
prophet of God. Has this changed since your administration?

WDM: Certainly, the Honorable Elijah Muhammad,
the way he discussed his own messianic prophet
image, made it possible for us to reestablish the Honorable Elijah Muhammad as a minister. In the early
days, and this is on record, he was called first minister of the Nation of Islam. That's why when I assumed the position of leadership, I took on the name
of Chief Minister which means first minister.
    The Honorable Elijah Muhammad on many occa-
sions said, "I am not a prophet. I am like the mailman. The mailman has a letter for you. That's
your letter; he has to give it to you." He had a
message to give. The Honorable Elijah Muhammad
didn't speak in the same theological spirit as the
Bible and Koran speak in. He talked of himself as
a messenger of God. He played down that supernatural experience. The Honorable Elijah Muhammad
said, "I am not a prophet but I am a messenger of
God." I think what he was trying to say was [he]
didn't get a revelation like Moses or Christ or like
Muhammad and the other great prophets. [He] got

a message in the ordinary sense.   Like you get a
letter from your friend or boss.
    The Honorable Elijah Muhammad didn't fix his
image in the minds of his people in such a scriptural
way that it couldn't be undone.   What I have done is
simply talk on the double meaning of Elijah Muhammad's teachings.   Elijah Muhammad was a student of
the Bible; his father was a Baptist minister.   That's
why Fard Muhammad chose him, because he was so
learned in the Bible.   The people were already Bible-
oriented.   There were other reasons, too, I guess.
The Bible called the preacher a messenger of God.
Honorable Elijah Muhammad was speaking in a common language, the daily spoken language and Bible
references.   He was not speaking from Koranic context.   He was saying, "A man came to me with solutions for your health problems, social problems,
and I bring you the message he gave to me."

CEM: What is the status of women in the organization since your administration?

WDM: We have tried to reexamine the role of women
in Al-Islam.   What I've done is study the treatment
of women during the early rise of Islam under prophet Muhammad himself and the early rulers to succeed
prophet Muhammad.   I have come to the conclusion
that prophet Muhammad and the Koran saw the women
in a different way than most Muslims see the women.
They have rights to equal education.   This was done
during the lifetime of prophet Muhammad.   During
his lifetime, women were given the right to engage
in business to compete with men and to hire men.
The rights of women to equal education were protected by Islam during the days of prophet Muhammad.
    I have looked at the role of women in that light--
in the light of what prophet Muhammad did, to give
more freedom, more equality to women.   I have come
to the conclusion that actually in our religion, we
cannot make any distinction between man and woman
in terms of intelligence, spirituality or nature.   Morally and intellectually speaking, women are equal with
men and they are not to be treated any differently.
They are to engage in business, to own wealth, to
own property.   They are to be allowed to excel in
academic pursuits.   If women are given freedom to
excel in academic pursuits, how can we tell them to

stay home? What is all this education for? You
can't keep her at home to nurse babies. I think all
we have to do is to study the treatment of women by
prophet Muhammad himself to understand what the
World Community of Al-Islam has done.

At one time we had a woman who was Plant Su-
pervisor. She was head of the Muhammad Speaks
plant under my own leadership. We have women in
key positions in the Masjid. We don't call them
Imams, we call them "Instructress." They teach the
religion, they propagate just like we do.

CEM: Are members required to use an X as their
last name anymore?

WDM: No. Again, that was the play on the power
of mystery to contain people. The X was a curiosity; it was a mystery. It made us feel we had something nobody else had. We don't need that anymore.
We don't have it.

CEM: The Honorable Elijah Muhammad and his son
Emmanuel served time in prison from 1942 to 1946.
Was this an asset or liability to the movement?
What role did Mrs. Clara Muhammad play during this
time?

WDM: The Honorable Elijah Muhammad introduced
a new outlook to his temples when he returned in
1946. The early followers were told not to listen
to radio. They were told to get all their education
in the temple. When the Honorable Elijah Muhammad
returned from prison, we started to listen to the
radio; soon TV came out. He introduced TV to us.
Immediately upon his release, he said we have to
become broader in our thinking. We need to establish many more temples and we need to get into business. He came out of prison with a business mind.

During his incarceration, Mrs. Clara Muhammad
was the Supreme Secretary for the whole movement.
The order came from him to her to the ministers
and captains. Actually, she was like his second while
he was in prison. She was executing his decisions
while he was in prison. I've seen her give instructions to the ministers. I was a child about 9, 10,
11, 12 years old. I saw her give instructions to ministers. They would sometimes be in doubt how they

should carry them out; she would give them insights.
She was a very strong woman and she believed in
him. She also believed in his teacher, Fard Muhammad. She was the one who served his meals to him
most of the time during his stay with the Honorable
Elijah Muhammad. She had a personal kind of relationship with W. D. Fard. She had direct faith in
him; it wasn't faith introduced by the Honorable Elijah Muhammad. He saw in her someone who wouldn't
budge for anything. When I disagreed with my father
she would say, "What's wrong with you, boy? You
crazy?"

CEM: Why did you rename the Mosque in New York
City after Malcolm Shabazz?

WDM: Because I felt my own hurt was shared by
most of the members in the Nation of Islam.   I
couldn't accept that Minister Malcolm be written off.
He established himself. He was the greatest minister the Nation of Islam ever had, except for the Honorable Elijah Muhammad. I can't say he was greater
than the Honorable Elijah Muhammad. He was, in
my opinion and many other ministers', the most
faithful minister to the Honorable Elijah Muhammad
in the whole history of the Nation of Islam.

CEM: Was Malcolm Shabazz instrumental in some
of the changes taking place now?

WDM: Well, I feel that Minister Malcolm's contribution to the changes that took place in the Nation of
Islam goes further back than my own. When I was
a young man ... Malcolm X was an influence in my
life. The thing that distinguished Malcolm X among
the ministers was his individuality. Malcolm X was
converted in prison. He came right out of prison
and became a minister for the Honorable Elijah Muhammad. He didn't take on the thinking and behavior
of the old conservative ministerial body. When the
Honorable Elijah Muhammad saw this new blood he
was excited. He just gave Malcolm free reign to
preach his doctrine. The Honorable Elijah Muhammad
welcomed this new blood. He told the old ministerial
body, "I will never get anywhere with people like
you." He said, "All you do is teach the same thing
we taught in the thirites." He would say, "Look at

this young man"; he would brag on Malcolm. He
said, "He's in modern times, he knows how to help
me." Malcolm's new thinking, courage and youth
attracted most of the young people into following the
Honorable Elijah Muhammad and I was one of them.
I used to admire the way he would uncover our own
ignorance.

CEM: Who do you think assassinated Malcolm X?

WDM: I don't know; I can't identify people. All I
can say is I don't believe the Nation of Islam planned
the assassination of Malcolm X. I believe outsiders
assassinated Malcolm X and members were used.

CEM: How many members are in the World Community of Al-Islam in the West?

WDM: We haven't really made an effort to count the
membership since mid-1976. At that time we estimated a 40 percent increase. That was about a year
after I became the Chief Minister. We estimated
70,000 people who have really declared their faith,
but over 1 million live Muslim lives.

CEM: Recently you became the Ambassador-at-large
for the World Community of Al-Islam in the West.
Please explain why you did this and what is your
function now?

WDM: I was not satisfied with the response in the
ministerial body to my call for us to get out in the
broader community and let our contributions be known.
We are fighting the same evils that Christians are
fighting. We are not fighting our private war. It's
a common fight against all evils in society. I didn't
really feel the ministers were responding to that. I
felt I would serve our community best by getting in
the media and doing public speaking engagements. I
then took on that role. In fact, I have spoken outside the community more than I have spoken inside.

CEM: Your title is Chief Minister or President?

WDM: No. The title is still Imam, Chief Minister.
President--that title is used to preserve my own position of authority in the World Community of Al-Islam

in the West.   Some people have a habit of trying to
give me a purely spiritual role in the community.
They do this because they want to control or take
over funds.   We are aware of this and I think the
editors of the Bilalian News are aware of that, too.
We want the followers to know throughout the country
and the world that my leadership is not for prayers
only; it covers all the business of the World Community of Al-Islam in the West.

CEM: Are the Fruit of Islam and Muslim Girls in
Training still functioning?

WDM: No, not as separate bodies.   They are still
functioning as Muslim Women in Training.   We still
have sisters in propagations.   They teach Islamic
diet, Islamic dress code, ... Islamic family structure and women's behavior at home and in public.
They teach the same things they taught us before.
In the NOI you were a member of an MGT class and
you would have to attend so many meetings a month
on Thursday night, take sewing, cooking and exercise.
We don't have that kind of regimentation any more,
but the teachings we do have.   Anyone who wants to
know about Islamic diet is free to go to the Koran.
We have women who just spend their time teaching
the things that MGT and FOI taught.   We have men
who do the same thing for a male membership.   The
Imams take care of that.

CEM: In October of 1975, you met with President
Anwar Sadat in the Drake Hotel in Chicago.   How
long have you had this relationship?   Is it still in-
tact?

WDM: That was my first acquaintance with President
Sadat and I have since then had one contact with him.
That was through the minister of education.   I have
received good wishes from him and his Muslim hol-
iday greeting.   Within the last year, I haven't heard
any word from him and I haven't sent him any word.

CEM: What do you think of President Sadat's peace
agreement with Israel?

WDM: This is a very sensitive question for me.   At
the Islamic conference held in Morocco, the 10th Is-

lamic Conference, I spoke to some of the delegations in a private meeting. I told them that I felt the Islamic world leadership had much to gain from the political psychology of President Sadat. I felt a new psychology was needed. What he's doing is inviting his people to come away from an emotional response to the presence of Israel on Muslim land to a more philosophical and rational strategy. To them it may look like Uncle Tomism, but to me it looks like wisdom.

CEM: If you could look into the future, where do you see the World Community of Al-Islam in the West in the year 2000?

WDM: I hope the year 2000 the World Community of Al-Islam in the West will be called American Muslims. I hope Muslims will be so comfortable in America that we won't have to introduce any structure or anything, just be American Muslims.

CEM: Why did you change the University of Islam to the Clara Muhammad School?

WDM: Because those old names were inflated to give us a sense of superiority. There were no real universities. There were grade schools, elementary schools and high schools. There were never any university levels, except maybe in the way we might interpret some of the theological teachings. No one would get that kind of symbolism in religion except on a college or university level. But as for the general courses taught in the schools, we were never on a university level.

The schools ... had an aura of mystery. It was creating abnormal minds as well as normal minds. We had some people who thought they were different human beings from others. They couldn't compete on their level with others in the public schools but they felt they were superior--they couldn't be penetrated. These cases were very few, not many. We did have this problem, where so many people were locked up in their own private world of supreme science. It wasn't anything but elementary knowledge. They couldn't integrate with the general world's thinking.

CEM: Recently the World Community of Al-Islam in

the West received \$20 million for food processing.
How did that come about?

WDM: As a result of the World Community of Al-
Islam trying to make practical use and profit from
our business holdings.   Faced with management problems, we had to go outside for management help.   I
went to the office of minority business enterprises
here in Chicago.   Just a thought came to me, "You
are now explaining your religion in a way which will
gain acceptance in America, so why not go to them
for help?"   There is no reason to fear going outside
for help.   I said to myself, "This is the kind of
thinking I have to encourage in our membership."   I
told members, "We have people who are taking ad-
vantage of us; they come in and pretend to be pro-
fessionals and get us in a lot of mess."   I said,
"What we need to do is cut these people out, what
they're doing is claiming to be representatives for
us in the outer world."   I said, "I am going directly
to government agencies.   There are officials to aid
people like us, people who have property, ability,
some economic holdings, but don't have the knowledge and experience."

It wasn't anymore than a month after I said this,
that I actually went.   I got the yellow pages and went
looking.   I said, "There's got to be something."   I
found the Organization of Minority Business Enterprises in the telephone book and I called them.   I
said, "We have holdings, we can do a lot of good.
We employ a lot of people, but we ran into economic
problems.   I think if we can get some help, some
business advice, if we can use your resources, I
think we can make a profit out of some of these holdings and create more jobs."   I explained to them
that my business interest was mainly jobs.   I say
jobs, because profit and money in the bank mean
nothing unless it is wisely invested to create more
opportunities for people.   So I explained this to the
Organization of Minority Business Enterprises, to Mr.
Harold Johnson and Mr. Dave Vegan.   They seemed
to be waiting for us to approach them.   They were
happy we came to them.   They said, "We think we
can give you a lot of help."   They began to make con-
tacts in their organization.   We were introduced to
Mr. Blackwell, the National President at that time,
and to the members of the Department of Commerce

in Washington. The work progressed right along and
before we knew it, we had a contract with the army.

CEM: Do you have any final comments you would
like to make?

WDM: Yes, I do. I am a religious man and a religious leader. I try to represent the religion the
way the prophets represented religion. I think that
it is being true to the religion. The prophets Moses,
Jesus, and Muhammad were all champions of the moral life of the people. You have people losing faith
in the future of employment, business opportunities,
giving up and accepting crime, welfare or just idle-
ness. That's a major moral problem. We have to
respond as religious leaders, Christians, Jews, Muslims; we have to respond just as the prophets would
respond. We, too, can join with government and
religious leaders, all people who are trying to preserve the good life for the individual. That means
having the opportunity to earn a living with your own
individual resources; that is a requirement of life.
Work is sacred. If we can't find a way to give jobs
to every able-bodied man and woman who wants to
work, we are failing society morally.

CEM: I want to thank you for this interview. One
of the prerequisites of a scholar is to be objective.
I have tried to be objective and not interject any of
my biases. As a young boy growing up in Los Angeles, California, I had the opportunity to witness
Muslims in the community working, serving and propagating the religion. There was always a mystery
about the "Black Muslims." Even though we were ig-
norant of the organization, we all respected them.
As I grew older and traveled across the country and
observed what the organization was doing in urban
areas, I began to respect the individuals. During
the time I was doing this study, members of the organization have been warm, kind, sensitive and understanding. Members have opened their minds and
hearts to help me. I want you to know it is an honor
and privilege to research the World Community of
Al-Islam in the West and have the opportunity to interview you.

WDM: Thank you very much. I am proud of our

membership and every time I hear compliments like
that it makes me feel very comfortable as a leader
in this community.

DIRECTORY OF MASJIDS IN THE UNITED STATES AND ABROAD

ALABAMA

Anniston 36202
AMM Center
600 West 15th St.
P.O. Box 81

Birmingham 35207
Birmingham Masjid
3424 26th St. N.

Dothan 36303
AMM Center
616 West Powell St.

Huntsville 35810
AMM Center
4903 Roebuck Rd., N.W.

Mobile 36605
AMM Center
1559 Duval St.

Montgomery 36104
AMM Center
937 S. Hull St.

Opelika 36801
AMM Center
1323 Auburn St.

Tuscaloosa 35401
AMM Center
7th St. 22 Ave.

ARIZONA

Phoenix 85001
Masjid Jauharatul Islam
102 West South Mountain Ave.
P.O. Box 1230

Tucson 85712
AMM Center
1830 S. Park Ave.

ARKANSAS

Ft. Smith 72903
AMM Center
1725 Midland Blvd.

Little Rock 72203
AMM Center
1717 Wright Ave.

CALIFORNIA

Altadena/Pasadena 91001
AMM Center
3184 North Olive Ave.

Bakersfield 93304
AMM Center
1001 8th St.

CALIFORNIA (cont.)

Compton 90221
AMM Center
1300 East Palmer Ave.

Long Beach 90806
AMM Center
2104 Orange Ave.

Los Angeles 90011
Masjid Felix Bilal
4016 S. Central Ave.

Los Angeles 90043
AMM Center
5450 Crenshaw Blvd.

Mountain View 94941
AMM Center
779 East Evelyn St.

Oakland 94601
Masjid Muhammad
1652 47th Ave.

Riverside 92517
AMM Center
P.O. Box 5708

Sacramento 95817
Oak Park Community Center
3425 Sacramento Blvd.

San Diego 92102
AMM Center
2575 Imperial Ave.

San Francisco 94117
AMM Center
850 DaVisaderro St.

San Jose 95116
AMM Center
1220 East San Antonio

San Luis Obispo 93401
AMM Center
283 Buchon St.

Stockton 95207
AMM Center
8063 N. Eldorado Suite No. 1

COLORADO

Denver 80207
AMM Center
4438 Sherman St.

CONNECTICUT

Bridgeport 06607
AMM Center
P.O. Box 4297
20 Yar Mich Drive

Hartford 06120
Masjid Muhammad
3284 Main St.

New Haven 06511
Masjid Muhammad
64 Carmel St.

South Norwalk 06856
AMM Center
P.O. Box 41

Stamford 06902
AMM Center
109 Tresser Blvd. 3D

DELAWARE

Wilmington 19801
AMM Center
301 West Sixth St.

DISTRICT OF COLUMBIA

Washington 20001
Washington Masjid
1519 Fourth St. N. W.

FLORIDA

Daytona Beach 32014
AMM Center
P. O. Box 6273

Ft. Lauderdale 33311
Masjid Nykhettah Muhammad
278 S. W. 27th Ave.
P. O. Box 9473

Gainsville 32601
AMM Center
302 N. W. 4th Ave.

Jacksonville 32209
AMM Center
2242 Commonwealth Ave.

Miami 33127
Masjid Al Ansar
5245 N. W. 7th Ave.

Pensacola 32501
AMM Center
1513 W. Garden St.

St. Petersburg 33701
AMM Center
922 Ninth St. South

Tallahassee 32304
AMM Center
115 Bragg Dr.

Tampa 33675
AMM Center
6013 N. 40th St.
P. O. Box 75216

GEORGIA

Albany 31707
AMM Center
511 Lincoln Ave.

Athens 30601
AMM Center
2685 Danielville Rd.

Atlanta 30316
Atlanta Masjid
735 Fayetteville Rd. S. E.

Augusta 30901
AMM Center
612 Beaufort Ave.

Brunswick 31520
AMM Center
3202 Franklin Ave.

Columbus 30501
AMM Center
1261 Spring St.

Griffin 30223
AMM Center
315 N. 3rd St.
P. O. Box 1042

La Grange 30240
AMM Center
208 Hamilton St.

Macon 31204
AMM Center
2031 East Napier Ave.

Milledgeville 31061
AMM Center
151 West McIntosh

Newman 30263
AMM Center
12-F Highland Apts.

GEORGIA (cont.)

Savannah 31401
AMM Center
117 East 34th St.

ILLINOIS

Carbondale 62901
AMM Center
321 S. Cedarview

Champaign 61820
AMM Center
P.O. Box 1746

Chicago 60649
Masjid, Hon. Elijah
  Muhammad
7351 S. Stony Island Ave.

Chicago 60627
Roseland AMM Center
11356 S. Wentworth

Danville 61832
AMM Center
P.O. Box 244

Decatur 62521
AMM Center
255 E. Orchard

Evanston 60201
AMM Center
1609 Emerson

Lockport 60441
AMM Center
523 Oak Ave.

North Chicago 60064
AMM Center
11226 Sheridan Rd.

Peoria 61604
AMM Center
2312 North Ellis

Rockford 61101
AMM Center
210 Morgan St.

INDIANA

Ft. Wayne 46806
AMM Center
1024 Oxford St.

Gary 46807
Masjid Muhammad
1473 West 15th Ave.

Indianapolis 46205
Masjid Muhammad
2931 Central Ave.

Michigan City 46360
AMM Center
P.O. Box 629

Mt. Vernon 47620
AMM Center
513 W. 4th St.

IOWA

Des Moines 50314
AMM Center
P.O. Box 1432

KANSAS

Kansas City 66014
AMM Center
1902 Quindard

Wichita 67214
AMM Center
1508 New York

KENTUCKY

Lexington   40508
AMM Center
572 Georgetown St.

Louisville   40211
AMM Center
1142 St. 42 St.

LOUISIANA

Baton Rouge   70805
AMM Center
P.O. Box 53205

New Orleans   70113
Masjid of Al-Islam
2626 Magnolia St.

Shreveport   71109
AMM Center
2401 Milam St.
P.O. Box 9202

Slidell   70458
AMM Center
Rt. 5 Box 135 E.

MARYLAND

Baltimore   21217
Masjid Baltimore
514 Wilson Ave.

MASSACHUSETTS

Dorchester   20120
Masjid Muhammad
35 Intervale St.

Springfield   01109
Masjid Muhammad
495 Union St.   P.O. Box 398
Highland Station

Worchester   01609
Masjid Muhammad
195 Pleasant St.

MICHIGAN

Benton Harbor   49022
AMM Center
241 E. Main St.

Detroit   48206
Masjid Wali Muhammad
11529 Linwood Ave.

Flint   48505
Masjid Muhammad
402 E. Gillespie

Grand Rapids   49507
AMM Center
1229 Madison

Inkster   48141
AMM Center
27311 Phipps

Kalamazoo   49007
AMM Center
1009 North Westnedge

Lansing   48915
AMM Center
235 Lahoma St.

Muskegon Heights   49444
AMM Center
2444 Park St.

Saginaw   48601
Masjid Abeedur-Rahman
114 North 4th St.

MINNESOTA

Minneapolis 55409
Masjid Mujaddad
3759 4th Ave. South

St. Paul 55104
AMM Center
324 N. St. Albans Ave.

MISSISSIPPI

Biloxi 39530
AMM Center
$501\frac{1}{2}$ Keller Ave.

Hattiesburg 39401
AMM Center
903 Elizabeth Ave.

Jackson 39204
AMM Center
1208 Jones Ave.

MISSOURI

Kansas City 64130
Masjid Omar
2715 Swope Pkwy.

St. Louis 63106
Masjid Muhammad
1434 North Grand Blvd.

NEBRASKA

Lincoln 28503
AMM Center
P.O. Box 82054

Omaha 6811
AMM Center
2914 Parker

NEVADA

Las Vegas 89106
AMM Center
820 West Lakemead

NEW JERSEY

Asbury Park 07712
Masjid As-siddig
733 Cookman Ave.

Atlantic City 08404
Masjid Muhammad
107 N. Centre
P.O. Box 782

Camden 08103
AMM Center
910 Broadway

East Orange 07018
Islamic Center of East Orange
239 Central Ave.

Elizabeth 07207
Masjid Muhammad
P.O. Box 59

Jersey City 07305
Masjid Muhammad
297 Martin Luther King Dr.
P.O. Box 26

New Brunswick 08903
AMM New Brunswick
P.O. Box 1688

Newark 07103
Masjid Muhammad
257 South Orange Ave.

Plainfield 07060
Masjid Muhammad
321 Grant Ave.

NEW JERSEY (cont.)

Somerset 08873
AMM Center
382-C Hamilton St.

Trenton 08607
AMM Center
1001 East State St.
P. O. Box 2454

NEW YORK

Albany 12210
AMM Center
P. O. Box 907

Bronx 10452
Masjid Muhammad
936 Woody Crest Ave.

Brooklyn 14203
Masjid Muhammad
615 Michigan St.

Jamaica 11468
AMM Center
Queens/Corona/Jamaica
10501 Northern Blvd.

Middletown 10940
AMM Center
P. O. Box 364

New York 10026
Masjid Malcolm Shabazz
102 West 116th St.

Poughkeepsie 12607
AMM Center/Masjid
  Muhammad
P. O. Box 21

Rochester 14605
Masjid Muhammad
370 North St.

Syracuse 13224
AMM Center-Syracuse/Utica
843 Salt Springs Rd.

Utica 13501
AMM Center
1132 Howard Ave.

Wyandanch 11798
AMM Center
1647 Straigh Path

NORTH CAROLINA

Asheville 28807
AMM Center
P. O. Box 7371

Charlotte 28216
Masjid Charlotte
1230 Beattiesford Rd.

Durham 27701
Masjid Durham
1009 West Chapell Hills St.

Fayetteville 28301
AMM Center
430 Gillespie St.

Greensboro 27401
AMM Center
1930 E. Market St.
P. O. Box 6201

Greenville 27834
AMM Center
917 Dickerson Ave.
P. O. Box 1044

Raleigh 27610
AMM Center
420 Hill St.

Statesville 28677
AMM Center
525 S. Center St.

NORTH CAROLINA (cont.)

Wilmington 28401
AMM Center
719½ Castle St.

Winston-Salem 27105
AMM Center
1500 English St.

OHIO

Akron 44320
AMM Center
875 Garth Ave.

Cincinnati 45207
Masjid Muhammad
Clarion and Trimble Ave.

Cleveland 44104
Masjid Willie Muhammad
2813 East 92nd St.

Columbus 43205
AMM Center
1677 Oak St.
P.O. Box 7048

Dayton 45401
AMM Center
P.O. Box 244

Lima 45805
AMM Center
435 S. Collette St.

Marion 43302
AMM Center
431 Evan Rd.

Sandusky 44870
AMM Center
P.O. Box 2381

Springfield 45506
AMM Center
743 Liberty St.

Toledo 43601
AMM Center
P.O. Box 426

Youngstown 44503
AMM Center
131 W. Woodland Ave.

OKLAHOMA

Lawton 73520
AMM Center
P.O. Box 2134

Oklahoma City 73111
AMM Center
1322 N.E. 23rd St.

Tulsa 74106
Al Baaqi Ar Rashid Center
538 East Oklahoma St.

OREGON

Portland 97211
AMM Center
5640 N.E. Union Ave.

PENNSYLVANIA

Chester 19013
AMM Center
19 West Third St.

Harrisburg 17103
AMM Center
1725 Market St.

PENNSYLVANIA (cont.)

Philadelphia 19122
Masjid Philadelphia
1319 West Susquehanna Ave.

Philadelphia 19150
Masjid Ul-llah
7511 Stenton Ave.

Pittsburgh 15208
AMM Center
7222 Kelly St.

RHODE ISLAND

Providence 02905
Masjid Muhammad
234 Pavillion Ave.

SOUTH CAROLINA

Anderson 29621
AMM Center
1998 Hugo Ave.

Columbia 29203
Columbia Masjid
5119 Monticello Rd.

Florence 29501
AMM Center
410 N. Coit St.

Moncks Corner 29461
AMM Center
Rt. 3 Box 43 B

Orangeburg 29115
AMM Center
P.O. Box 314

Rock Hill 29730
AMM Center
431 Gettys St.

TENNESSEE

Chattanooga 37404
AMM Center
504 Kilmer St.

Knoxville 37921
AMM Center
709 College St.

Memphis 38109
Memphis Masjid
4412 S. 3rd St.

Nashville 37209
AMM Center
3317 Torbett St.

TEXAS

Austin 78744
AMM Center
P.O. Box 18812

Beaumont 77704
AMM Center
P.O. Box 2008

Dallas 75215
Masjid of Al-Islam
2604 S. Hardwood

El Paso 79904
AMM Center
9000 Marks-Apt. 31

Ft. Worth 76104
Hassan Center
1201 East Allen Ave.

Houston 77087
Masjid of Al-Islam
6641 Bellfort Ave.

Lubbock 79401
AMM Center
P.O. Box 5842

TEXAS (cont.)

Port Arthur   77640
AMM Center
615 East 5th St.

San Antonio   78202
AMM Center
1702 Hays St.

Tyler   75702
AMM Center
520 West Bowist

VIRGINIA

Martinsville   24112
AMM Center
1011 W. Fayette St.

Newport News   23607
AMM Center
1145 Hampton Ave.

Norfolk   24016
AMM Center
1106-08 East 26th St.

Petersburg   23805
AMM Center
1103 West Washington St.

Richmond   23223
AMM Center
400 Chimborazo Blvd.
P.O. Box 8064

Roanoke   24016
AMM Center
822 Campbell Ave. S.W.

WASHINGTON

Seattle   98118
P.O. Box 18375
Mt. Baker Community Hall
2811 Mt. Ranier Dr. South

Tacoma   98405
AMM Center
2523 S. Ainsworth

WEST VIRGINIA

Charleston   23525
AMM Center
P.O. Box 1124

WISCONSIN

Milwaukee   53212
Masjid Sultan Muhammad
2507 N. 3rd St.

Racine   53404
Masjid Muhammad
815 Silver St.

OUTSIDE THE UNITED STATES

Nassau, Bahamas
Masjid Muhammad Nassau
P.O. Box N3232

Bridgetown, Barbados
Masjids Muhammad Barbados
c/o Husbands of Barbados
Spry St.

OUTSIDE THE UNITED
STATES (cont.)

Belize City, Belize
Masjid Muhammad Belize
10 Race Course St.

Hamilton, Bermuda 5
Masjid Muhammad--Bermuda
Cedar Ave. P. O. Box 1508

Montreal, Quebec, Canada
Fatima Mosque
2012 St. Dominque

Georgetown, Guyana
Masjid Muhammad Guyana
47 Robb St. Borda
P. O. Box 24 G. P. O.

Downsvien, Ontario N 3N2TI
Canada
Masjid Muhammad
P. O. Box 2243 Toronto Station C

Kingston, Jamaica
Masjid Muhammad Jamaica
Central Sorting Office
P. O. Box 8045

St. Mary, Jamaica
Masjid Muhammad
9 Kirk St.
Port Maria

Charlotte Amalie
Masjid Muhammad
St. Thomas, U. S. V. I.
P. O. Box 2548

Republic of Trinidad and Tobago
Masjid Muhammad
Trinidad
44-48 Park Street

BIBLIOGRAPHY

BOOKS

Ali, Drew N. The Holy Koran of the Moorish Holy Temple
of Science. Chicago: Moorish Science Temple, 1914.

Apter, David E., ed. Ideology and Discontent. New York:
Markham, 1972.

Ash-Garner, Roberta. Social Movements in America. Chicago: Rand-McNally, 1977.

_____. Social Change. Chicago: Rand-McNally, 1977.

Barbeau, Arthur E., and Henry Florette. The Unknown Soldiers. Philadelphia: Temple University Press, 1974.

Bennett, Lerone. Pioneers of Protest. Chicago: Johnson,
1968.

Bishai, Wilson B. Humanities in the Arab-Islamic World.
New York: Wm C. Brown, 1973.

Bontemps, Arna. Anyplace But Here. New York: Hill and
Wang, 1966.

_____, and Jack Conroy. They Seek a City. New York:
Doubleday, 1945.

Boskin, Joseph. Urban Racial Violence in the Twentieth Cen-
tury. Beverly Hills, Cal.: Glencoe Press, 1969.

Bracey, John H., and August Meier. Black Nationalism in
America. New York: Bobbs-Merrill, 1970.

Brown, Michael, and Amy Golden. Collective Behavior.
Pacific Palisades, Cal.: Goodyear, 1973.

Blyden, Edward W. Pan-Negro Patriot. London: Oxford
University Press, 1967.

Carmichael, Stokely, and Charles V. Hamilton. Black Power.
New York: Vintage Books, 1967.

Clarke, John H., ed. Marcus Garvey and the Vision of Africa. New York: Vintage Books, 1974.

Cleage, Albert B. Black Christian Nationalism. New York:
William Morrow, 1972.

Cox, Oliver. Caste, Class and Race. New York: Doubleday,
1948.

Cronon, Edmond D. Black Moses. Madison: University of
Wisconsin Press, 1966.

Cruse, Harold. The Crisis of the Negro Intellectual. New
York: William Morrow, 1967.

Cushmeer, Bernard. This Is the One. Phoenix, Ariz.:
Truth Publications, 1970.

Dalfiume, Richard M. Desegregation of the U.S. Armed
Forces. Columbia: University of Missouri Press, 1969.

David, Fay, and Elaine Crane. The Black Soldiers. New
York: William Morrow, 1971.

Delaney, Martin. The Condition, Elevation, Emigration and
Destiny of the Colored People of the United States, Politically Considered. New York: Arno Press, 1968.

Draper, Theodore. The Rediscovery of Black Nationalism.
New York: Viking Press, 1969.

Drotning, Phillip T. Black Heroes in Our Nation's History.
New York: Cowles Books, 1969.

Du Bois, W.E.B. Black Folk: Then and Now. New York:
Octagon Book, 1939.

_____. Dark Princess. New York: Harcourt, Brace,
1928.

_____. Souls of Black Folk, Greenwich, Conn.   Fawcett
Premier Book, 1961.

_____. The World and Africa.   New York: Viking Press,
1947.

Essien-Udom, E. U.   Black Nationalism: A Search for an Identity in America.   Chicago: University of Chicago Press,
1962.

Factor, Robert L.   The Black Response to America.   Reading, Mass.:   Addison-Wesley, 1970.

Fauset, Arthur F.   Black Gods of the Metropolis.   Philadelphia: University of Pennsylvania Press, 1944.

Fax, Elson C.   Garvey, The Story of a Pioneer Black Nationalist.   New York: Dodd, Mead, 1972.

Feuer, Lewis S., ed.   Marx and Engles.   Garden City, N.Y.:
Anchor Books, 1969.

Foner, Jack D.   Blacks and the Military in American History.
New York: Praeger, 1974.

Franklin, John H.   From Slavery to Freedom.   New York:
Random House, 1969.

Garvey, Amy J., ed.   Philosophy and Opinions of Marcus
Garvey.   New York: Athenaeum Press, 1969.

Gerth, H., and C. Wright Mills, eds.   From Max Weber Es-
says in Sociology.   New York: Oxford University Press,
1968.

Grant, Joanne, ed.   Black Protest History, Documents and
Analysis 1619 to the Present.   Greenwich, Conn.:   Fawcett, 1968.

Greene, Robert E.   Black Defenders of America 1775-1973.
Chicago: Johnson, 1974.

Grimshaw, Allen, ed.   Racial Violence in the United States.
Chicago: Aldine, 1969.

Groh, George W.   The Black Migration.   New York: Weybright and Talley, 1972.

Gusfield, Joseph H. Protest, Reform and Revolt. New York: John Wiley and Sons, 1970.

Hall, Ray, ed. Black Separatism and Social Reality. New York: Pergamon Press, 1977.

Haley, Alex. Roots. New York: Doubleday, 1976.

Heberle, Rudolph. Social Movements. New York: Appleton-Century-Crofts, 1951.

Henri, Florette. Black Migration Movement North. 1900-1920. New York: Anchor Press, 1975.

Heywood, Chester D. Negro Combat Troops in the World War. New York: Negro Universities Press, 1928.

Killian, Lewis M., and Ralph H. Turner. Collective Behavior. Englewood Cliffs, N.J.: Prentice-Hall, 1957.

Krauss, Irving. Stratification Class and Conflict. New York: The Free Press, 1976.

Lang, Kurt, and Gladys E. Lang. Collective Dynamics. New York: Thomas Y. Crowell, 1961.

Lebon, Gustav. The Crowd. New York: Ballantine Books, 1969.

Lincoln, Eric C. The Black Muslims in America. Canada: Saunders of Toronto, 1961.

Lynch, Hollis. Edward Wilmont Blyden. London: Oxford University Press, 1967.

Marx, Karl. A Contribution to the Critique of Political Economy. Chicago: Charles Hikerr, 1904.

_____. The Economic and Philosophic Manuscript of 1844. New York: International, 1972.

Miller, Donald L. Black Americans in the Armed Forces. New York: Franklin Watts, 1969.

Mills, C. Wright. Power, Politics and People. New York: Ballantine Books, 1963.

Mitchell, Paul, ed. Race Riots in Black and White. Englewood Cliffs, N.J.: Prentice-Hall, 1970.

Muhammad, Elijah. How to Eat to Live. Chicago: Muhammad Mosque No. 2, 1972.

_____. Message to the Black Man in America. Chicago: Muhammad Mosque No. 2, 1965.

_____. The Supreme Wisdom: Solution to The So-Called Negroe's Problem. Chicago: University of Islam, 1957.

Myrdal, Gunnar. An American Dilemma. New York: Harper and Brothers, 1944.

Oberschall, Anthony. Social Conflict and Social Movements. Englewood Cliffs, N.J.: Prentice-Hall, 1973.

Parkin, Frank. Class Inequality and Political Order. New York: Praeger Press, 1972.

Perlo, Victor. Economics of Racism U.S.A. New York: International, 1975.

Plaft, Anthony. The Politics of Riot Commission. 1917-1970. New York: Macmillan, 1971.

Raper, Arthur G. Preface to Peasantry. Chapel Hill: University of North Carolina Press, 1936.

Redkey, Edwin S. Black Exodus, Black Nationalism and Back to Africa Movements 1890-1910. New Haven, Conn.: Yale University Press, 1969.

Roberts, Ron E., and Robert Kloss. Social Movements Between the Balcony and the Barricade. Saint Louis, Mo.: C.V. Mosby, 1974.

Rudwick, Elliott M. Race Riot in East St. Louis, 1917. Carbondale: Southern Illinois University Press, 1964.

Schoenfeld, Seymour J. The Negro in the Armed Forces. Washington, D.C.: The Associated Publishers, 1945.

Scott, Emmett J. Scott's Official History of the American Negro in the World War. Chicago: L.W. Walters, 1919.

Simpson, George E., and Milton J. Yinger. Racial and Cultural Minorities. New York: Harper and Row, 1965.

Smelser, Neil J. Theory of Collective Behavior. New York: The Free Press, 1962.

Sternsher, Bernard. The Negro in Depression and War. Chicago: Quandrangle Books, 1969.

Sweeney, Allison W. History of the American Negro in the Great World War. New York: Johnson Reprint Corporation, 1970.

Terraine, John. The Great War 1914-1918. New York: Macmillan, 1965.

Turner, Ralph H., and Lewis M. Killian. Collective Behavior. Englewood Cliffs, N.J.: Prentice-Hall, Inc., 1972.

Vincent, Theodore G. Black Power and the Garvey Movement. Berkeley, Calif.: Ramparts Press, 1972.

Wagstaff, Thomas, ed. Black Power, the Radical Response to White America. Beverly Hills, Cal.: The Glencoe Press, 1969.

Wakin, Edward. Black Fighting Men in U.S. History. New York: Lothrop, Lee and Shepard, 1971.

Waskow, Arthur I. From Race Riot to Sit In, 1919 and the 1960's. Garden City, N.Y.: Doubleday, 1966.

Weber, Max. The Theory of Social and Economic Organization. New York: Oxford University Press, 1977.

Wilson, Christy J. Introducing Islam. New York: Friendship Press, 1975.

Woofter, Thomas J. Negro Migration. New York: Negro Universities Press, 1969.

X, Malcolm, and Alex Haley. Autobiography of Malcolm X. New York: Grove Press, Inc., 1964; New York: Ballantine Books, 1973, 1977.

GOVERNMENT DOCUMENTS

Bureau of Education. Negro Education in the United States. Washington, D.C.: Government Printing Office, 1917.

Bureau of the Census. Changing Characteristics of the Negro Population. Washington, D.C.: Government Printing Office, 1969.

Bureau of the Census. Negro Population in the United States 1790-1915. Washington, D.C.: Government Printing Office, 1918.

Bureau of the Census. Negroes in the United States, 1920-1932. Washington, D.C.: Government Printing Office, 1935.

Chief of the Statistics Branch of the General Staff. The War with Germany. Washington, D.C.: Government Printing Office, 1919.

Committee on Classification of Personnel in the United States Army. History of the Personnel System. 2 vols. Washington, D.C.: Government Printing Office, 1919.

Department of Interior. The Urban Negro Worker in the United States 1925-1936. Washington, D.C.: Office of the Secretary, 1934.

Department of Labor. Negro Migration in 1916-1917. Washington, D.C.: Government Printing Office, 1919.

Federal Bureau of Investigation. The Black Muslim Movement. Washington, D.C.: U.S. Department of Justice, 1973.

Federal Bureau of Investigation. The Nation of Islam. Washington, D.C.: U.S. Department of Justice, 1960.

Federal Bureau of Investigation. Nation of Islam, Cult of the Black Muslims. Washington, D.C.: U.S. Department of Justice, 1965.

Historical Section, Army War College. Order of Battle of the United States Land Forces in the World War. Washington, D.C.: Historical Section, Army War College, Government Printing Office, 1931.

Lee, Ulysses. The Employment of Negro Troops, U.S. Army in the World War II. Washington, D.C.: Office of the Chief of Military History, United States Army, 1966.

Second Report, Provost Marshal General to the Secretary of War. On the Operations of the Selective Service System to December 20, 1918. Washington, D.C.: Government Printing Office, 1919.

JOURNALS

Beynon, Erdmann D. "The Negro Cult Among Negro Migrants in Detroit." American Journal of Sociology, 6 (May 1938): 894-907.

Du Bois, W.E.B. "An Essay Toward a History of the Black Man in the Great War." The Crisis, 18 (May-October 1919).

Hatchett, John F. "The Muslim Influence Among American Negroes." Journal of Human Relations, 10 (Summer 1962): 375.

Karenga, Ron M. "Afro-American Nationalism, Beyond Mystification and Misconception." Black Books Bulletin, vol. 6, no. 1 (Spring 1979).

_____. "A Strategy for Struggle: Turning Weakness into Strength." The Black Scholar, 5 (November 1975): 15-19.

Scott, Emmett J. "The Participation of Negroes in World War I." Journal of Negro Education, XIII (Summer 1943).

Turner, James. "Blyden, Black Nationalism and Emigration Schemes." Black Books Bulletin, vol. 6, no. 1 (Spring 1979).

PHONOGRAPH RECORDS

Farrakhan, Louis. "Black Family Day." New York: Nation of Islam Recording, P.O. Box 2231, May 27, 1974.

Muhammad, Elijah. "Muslim Wants and Beliefs." Chicago: Produced by Muhammad's Mosque of Islam No. 2, no date.

_____. "Speaking of Judgement." Chicago: Produced by
Muhammad's Mosque of Islam No. 2, no date.

_____. "The Time and What Must Be Done." Chicago:
Produced by Muhammad's Mosque of Islam No. 2, no date.

NEWSPAPERS

Bilalian News. November 21, 1975.

Bilalian News. October 24, 1976.

Muhammad Speaks. Special Issue, April 1972.

New York Post. February 23, 1965.

New York Post. February 28, 1965.

Pittsburgh Courier. January 18, 1958.

Pittsburgh Courier. March 6, 1965, p. 4.

UNPUBLISHED MATERIAL

Hall, Raymond. "Black Separatist Movements." Ph. D.
dissertation, Syracuse University, 1972.

Nation of Islam. "The Muhammad Appreciation Day Journal."
Pamphlet. Chicago: Nation of Islam Publication, June
1975.

Nation of Islam. "The Nation of Islam in Action." Pamphlet.
Chicago: Nation of Islam Publication, 1976.

PUBLIC ADDRESS

Farrakhan, Louis. "The Nation of Islam." Virginia Union
University Student Assembly, Richmond, Virginia, February
4, 1976.

Muhammad, Wallace. "Public address." Richmond, Virginia:
Temple No. 24, April 1, 1977.

INTERVIEWS

Charles 4X Jackson, Member of Nation of Islam, Los Angeles, California, April 4, 1971.

Sam Bey, Member of Moorish Science Temple, Richmond, Virginia, November 12, 1975.

Sharon Shabazz, Curator of Master Elijah Muhammad Library, New York City, December 16, 1975.

Kareem Muhammad, Member of World Community of Al-Islam in the West, New York City, December 22, 1975.

Alif Muhammad, Member of Nation of Islam, Washington, D. C. June 6, 1976.

James 2X Jones, Member of Nation of Islam, Richmond, Virginia, July 5, 1976.

George Bey, Minister of Moorish Science Temple No. 6, Richmond, Virginia, August 4, 1976.

Bill El, Member of Moorish Science Temple, Richmond, Virginia, August 4, 1976.

Fatima El, Member of Moorish Science Temple, Richmond, Virginia, August 4, 1976.

Karen El, Member of Moorish Science Temple, Richmond, Virginia, August 4, 1976.

Frank Bey, Member of Moorish Science Temple, Richmond, Virginia, August 10, 1976.

Benjamin 4X Jackson, Member of Nation of Islam, Richmond, Virginia, April 1, 1977.

Muhammad Akbar, Muslim Official World Community of Al-Islam in the West, Telephone interview, April 21, 1977.

Wallace Muhammad, Chief Minister of World Community of Al-Islam in the West, Chicago, Illinois, July 25, 1979.

INDEX